CW00418269

The Stealing OF THE *Irish Crown Jewels*

AN UNSOLVED CRIME

The Stealing OF THE *Irish Crown Jewels*

AN UNSOLVED CRIME

by

MYLES DUNGAN

TOWN HOUSE
DUBLIN

First published in 2003 by

TownHouse, Dublin
THCH Ltd
Trinity House
Charleston Road
Ranelagh
Dublin 6
Ireland

1 2 3 4 5 6 7 8 9 10

A CIP catalogue record for this book is available from the British Library.

ISBN: 1-86059-182-5

Cover and text design by Anú Design, Tara
Typeset by Anú Design, Tara
Printed by Rotanor, Norway 2003

Contents

✍ Act Three ~ *Denouement*

✍ Epilogue

for Emma

Acknowledgements

The perpetrators of one of the most intriguing and mysterious crimes of early-20th century Ireland are safely in their graves. No documentary evidence exists that conclusively identifies them so, if you are a reader who likes a beginning, middle and neatly tied-up end to a story, read no further.

The subject of this book is little more than an entertaining and intriguing footnote in Irish history, though it does have a hallowed place in the annals of Irish crime. I have tried to write a readable account of a complex and involved subject. Where I might appear to be venturing an unsupported opinion on the state of mind or the thinking of some protagonists, there is ample evidence in the testimony to the invaluable Viceregal Commission of Investigation into the theft, to justify what may appear to be speculation on my part. However, I have taken the liberty of assuming that the reader will have some trust in the author and will not require footnotes and constant source references. The provenance of most quotations and assertions is indicated in the text. For those so inclined, there is a section on sources on *page 279*.

I have corresponded over the years in the preparation of this work with Reverend Peter Galloway, Liam T Cosgrave, the Earl of Granard, Senator Maurice Manning, Margery Fisher (co-author of *Shackleton*), Desmond Fitzgerald, Garret FitzGerald and Lord Moyne.

My gratitude is due to the staffs of the various libraries where I have conducted research, most notably the National Library of Ireland, the

Genealogical Office, the Public Record Office, the State Paper Office, the British Library, the Public Record Office in Kew, Sir Robin Mackworth Young and Mr Oliver Everett of the Royal Archive in Windsor and M M White of the Home Office Departmental Records Office in London. Ms Helen Langley and R K Francis of the Bodleian Library in Oxford rendered a trip there unnecessary.

A particular word of thanks is due to Ken Stone of the Metropolitan Police Museum – I now reluctantly conclude that, if Inspector Kane's report ever made it to the museum it is certainly not there now!

I'm grateful to the then editor of *The Irish Times*, Douglas Gageby, and the then features editor, Brian Fallon, for printing a long article on the subject of the theft in 1982. This put me on to the James Weldon story thanks to a subsequent 'Letter to the Editor'.

My thanks to Treasa Coady of TownHouse for enabling me to return to something I started a long time ago and put aside to do other things, as well as to Marie Heaney for struggling through a first draft that I thought was far more readable than it subsequently turned out to be. Claire Rourke has patiently taken me through a further draft with many extremly apposite questions and observations. I am also grateful to my friend and American travelling companion Stacey Jones for her comments and to my daughter Lara for hers (and for allowing me to be her proud Dad).

And to the few people who, for various reasons, would prefer not to have their help and co-operation acknowledged, thank you anyway!

Myles Dungan
August 2003

Prologue

THE JEWELS THAT King William IV chose to donate to the Order of St Patrick in 1831 had had a chequered history. By the time they were presented to the Order, they had already belonged to no less than two royal mistresses. Their provenance was appropriate – because now they were being bestowed largely as an enticement to Irish noblemen to offer their unstinting support to the crown.

William IV was the least unpopular of King George III's disagreeable and dissolute sons. Not that his sex life was any more orthodox than that of his brothers. When duty called, he had reluctantly agreed to end a lengthy affair with a well-known actress in order to father a child by his wife Adelaide, an obscure German princess. In the event, he fathered no children and continued the affair anyway. His wife turned out to be an appealing and tolerant woman and she certainly needed to be. It is rumoured that the eccentric King actually used to entertain his mistress and her children to dinner once a week – Queen Adelaide would dine with them, placing herself at one end of the table, her husband at the other, with the actress, *en famille*, in the centre.

But when it came to the jewels, even the long-suffering Queen Adelaide's patience snapped. William offered them to her as a gift but, when she was told something of their history, she was less than flattered. They had been presented by William's brother, George IV, to two consecutive paramours. When the King had died, they had been returned, with extraordinary delicacy, by the second mistress. On being made aware of this, Queen Adelaide rebelled. Perhaps she felt that they would have been more appropriately offered to King William's mistress rather than his wife. At any rate the King didn't give them to the actress. He did what one would expect any English monarch to do with something so troublesome – he sent them to Ireland.

The Most Illustrious Order of St Patrick, established in 1783, was a highly exclusive club. Its members boasted the bluest blood in the land, St Patrick's blue, the official colour of the Order. Its officers included the Lord Lieutenant and the Church of Ireland Primate and its functions graced the most sumptuous rooms of Dublin Castle. But it lacked official regalia on a par with that of its fraternal British orders – the Garter, Thistle and Bath. Once again, the Irish were the poor relations. King William's gift rectified this oversight – although, ironically, his jewels would not be worn by an Irishman.

The Lord Lieutenant, as Grand Master of the Order of St Patrick, was entitled to wear the Insignia of the Order on ceremonial occasions. As the King's man in Ireland, it was felt that his regalia should be somewhat more ornate than that of any of the individual knights. It was decided to use King William's gems to provide him with a jewelled Star and Badge.

The work of creating the insignia was done by the London firm of Rundell, Bridge and Rundell, based in Ludgate Hill. They fashioned a Star measuring five inches by four, with eight points, consisting of Brazilian white diamonds. In the centre was a cross of rubies on a trefoil of emeralds, which was meant to represent a shamrock. This was surrounded by a sky-blue enamel circle with the motto of the order 'Quis Separabit?' and the date of its inception 'MDCCLXXXIII' inscribed in tiny rose diamonds.

The Badge was set in silver – smaller than the Star but more elabo-rate, measuring about three inches by two and a half. The centre was similar to the centre of the Star except it was more oblong in shape but, once again, the cross was of rubies and the trefoil of emeralds. Outside, the sky-blue enamelled circle was a ring of large Brazilian diamonds. All this was topped off by a three-inch crowned harp of small Brazilian white diamonds. Officially, the entire ensemble bore the impressive title of 'The Insignia of the Grand Master of the Order of St Patrick'; col-loquially, this remarkable assortment of gems became the 'Irish Crown Jewels'.

They still belonged to the Order of St Patrick when they were last seen, intact, on 11th June 1907.

Dramatis Personae

ARGYLL, DUKE OF: Married to Princess Louise,
                      sister of King Edward VII

ABERDEEN, LORD: John Campbell Gordon, Lord
                      Lieutenant (King's representative
                      in Ireland)

BARRY, REDMOND: Solicitor General

BENNETT GOLDNEY, FRANCIS: Athlone Pursuivant,
                      Mayor of Canterbury

BIRRELL, AUGUSTINE: Chief Secretary for Ireland and
                      member of the British cabinet

BURTCHAELL, GEORGE: Genealogist and the Office of
                      Arms Secretary

DOUGHERTY, SIR JAMES: Assistant Under Secretary for
                      Ireland (1907) and
                      Under Secretary (1908)

EDWARD VII, KING: Reigned 1901–1910

FARRELL, MARY:	Office of Arms cleaner
GIBBON, MARY:	Office of Arms typist
GINNELL, LAURENCE:	Nationalist MP for Westmeath
GORGES, RICHARD:	Militia Captain and associate of Francis Shackleton
GOWER, LORD RONALD:	Uncle of the Duke of Argyll and associate of Shackleton
HADDO, LORD GEORGE:	Son of Lord Aberdeen
HARRELL, M V:	Assistant Commissioner of the Dublin Metropolitan Police
HIRD, FRANK:	Adopted son of Gower and defrauded by Shackleton
HOBSON, BULMER:	Republican activist and Dublin journalist
HODGSON, J C:	Antiquary and associate of Sir Arthur Vicars
HOLMES, SIR GEORGE:	Chairman of the Board of Works
HORLOCK, SYDNEY:	Sir Arthur Vicars' Private Secretary

KANE, JOHN:	Inspector of the London Metropolitan Police, Scotland Yard
KERR, OWEN:	Detective of the Dublin Metropolitan Police
KNOLLYS, LORD:	King Edward VII's secretary
LOWE, JOHN:	Superintendent of the Dublin Metropolitan Police
MACDONNELL, SIR ANTHONY:	Under Secretary for Ireland, second in rank to Birrell
MAHONY, PIERCE GUN:	Cork Herald and nephew of Sir Arthur Vicars
O'MAHONY, PIERCE:	Former nationalist MP, half-brother and defender of Vicars
ROSS, SIR JOHN:	Commissioner of the Dublin Metropolitan Police
SHACKLETON, FRANCIS:	Dublin Herald and brother of the polar explorer, Ernest
STIVEY, WILLIAM:	Office of Arms messenger

VICARS, SIR ARTHUR: Ulster King of Arms, in charge
of the Office of Arms and official
keeper of the Irish Crown Jewels

WILKINSON, SIR NEVILLE: Vicars' successor as Ulster King
of Arms

Act One

Theft and Investigation

1

The Safe

The Bedford Tower, Dublin Castle, April 1903

THERE WAS ABSOLUTELY nothing Pemberton could do with the safe. No matter what the builder did, it was like trying to push a camel through the eye of a needle. It stood there, static and uncompromising, in the shambles of the old Fisheries building, its bulk blocking the entrance to the brand-new strong-room.

The strong-room itself measured fifteen feet by ten and was an impressive structure. The walls were virtually impenetrable. They were lined on the inside with fire-proof brick and the door was a steel monster weighing a couple of tons. Even though it wasn't his responsibility, Pemberton was happy with the door. It would take a few hundred pounds of dynamite to blow it off its hinges – if anyone was foolish enough to try using explosives in Dublin Castle. Inside the huge door was a grille. It was standing open, waiting for the safe to be wheeled in.

But the safe wouldn't budge. It had to pass through a two-foot gap and was nearly three feet wide. The builder and the men from the Board of Works, Thornton and Bent, had tried everything. At first, they had approached the opening directly, with the safe on casters – it had jammed. Then they had tried again, confidently, from an angle. Still no progress. After a few more sorties, and a few more retreats, they had given up, victims of the axiom that three into two won't go. It was hot and exhausting work and the Bedford Tower was full of stifling dust from the renovations. The arrival of the safe in the first place had come as a surprise to Pemberton as he had been told nothing about it. Bent and Thornton had simply appeared with instructions from Sir Arthur Vicars that it was to be put into the tower's newly built strong-room.

The tired and frustrated builder could see trouble on the horizon. But he had been given his own brief, as had the Milner Safe Company, who had built the strong-room door. Their orders had tallied. The door had fitted the space he had been told to leave. They were in the clear. The fault lay elsewhere.

He sent for Sir Arthur Vicars, the man who presided over the little heraldic bureau that was the Office of Arms; the man who bore the ancient title of Ulster King of Arms and for whom the Bedford Tower was being refurbished. The half dozen inhabitants of the Office of Arms, crammed together in three small rooms in the Bermingham Tower in the Lower Castle Yard, would soon be moving in. Consequently, the Bedford Tower was a mess – a separating wall had been knocked down to turn two small downstairs rooms into one larger one. This was being prepared to house a library, but now it looked as if the room would have to accommodate an unexpected guest, a squat but imposing safe that clearly was not going to go into the strong-room.

When Sir Arthur Vicars arrived, the situation was explained to him. A safe that was three feet wide could not be manhandled through a smaller opening. Vicars left abruptly. He was clearly incensed, but realised that it was pointless to direct his anger at the three men sitting in the Bedford Tower awaiting orders. He was gone for some time and, when he returned, it was clear that he had gone straight to the top. He was accompanied by Sir George Holmes, Chairman of the Board of Works, the official body charged with the upkeep of all government buildings.

Had he heard the conversation between the two men, Pemberton would have realised the importance of the safe. It was being used to protect the 'Crown Jewels'. The Board of Works had spent almost £300 building the strong-room and they were not in the habit of dispensing such large sums without good reason. Vicars was maintaining that he had given specific instructions that the safe was to be housed in the strong-room; Holmes was insisting that Vicars had not made that clear to anyone in the Board of Works. The assumption was that the strong-room would be *replacing* the safe as the repository for the jewels.

The argument continued thus, unabated and irreconcilable, as the temporarily redundant trio of Pemberton, Bent and Thornton awaited instructions.

Dublin Castle is a bit of a curate's egg – good in parts, but ugly and unprepossessing in others. It is a castle only in name. The River Poddle flows underneath its courtyards and, as a result, many of the buildings were inordinately damp at the turn of the 19th century. They also smelled. The Bermingham Tower, which offered some of the least comfortable accommodation in the Castle, had, in 1591, housed the great Irish Chieftain Hugh

O'Donnell when he had been an unwilling guest of Queen Elizabeth I. The amenities had been improved since his stay, but not sufficiently to satisfy Sir Arthur Vicars. He was the last-remaining working officer of the Order of St Patrick and was the expert genealogist who administered the Office of Arms. When he had learned that his working quarters were to be moved to the Bedford Tower in the more impressive Upper Castle Yard, he had been elated. The tower was a much more imposing pile – for a start, the brickwork didn't weep like that in his present accommodation.

Added to his pleasure at the grandeur of his new surroundings, Vicars was delighted for another reason. The Bedford Tower afforded greater security for the protection of the Grand Master's Insignia, the so-called Crown Jewels. It fell to Vicars to safeguard the jewels at all times and was not a duty he greatly cherished. It had come with the territory when he took up his post in 1893. Prior to his appointment, the practice had been to lodge the gems with the jewellers, West's of Grafton Street. Shortly before the insignia were required on ceremonial occasions by the Lord Lieutenant, they would be brought from West's and left in an iron box in a wall safe in the Bermingham Tower. The doors of this safe were made only of wood, the jewels would be far safer in the Bedford Tower.

After the absurd pas de deux between safe and strong-room, the usual quota of memos and correspondence flew backwards and forwards between the Board of Works and the Office of Arms. Each blamed the other for the debacle. Finally, gentlemen compromised where gentlemen should – in their club. Shortly after taking over occupancy of the Bedford Tower, Vicars bumped into Sir George Holmes in the Kildare Street Club. Vicars was in an expansive humour, he often became overgenerous after a few drinks. Everything, it appeared, was capable of resolution. Vicars was prepared to accept that, on reflection, there was no real need for the safe to be put in the strong-room – it would take up too much space there anyway – and so he agreed to its permanent residence in the office library.

It was an act of magnanimity that would come back to haunt him. So would a bureaucratic oversight untypical of the punctilious Vicars. In 1905, he revised the Statutes of the Order of St Patrick. Under the new regulations, the diamond insignia of the Order (officially described as 'Crown Jewels' under Article XII of the Statutes) were still to be 'deposited for safe keeping in a steel safe in the strong-room… of the Office of Arms'. Ulster King of Arms (namely Vicars himself) remained their designated custodian. Vicars could have changed the wording of the regulation or shifted himself to procure a smaller safe that would fit into the strong-room. He did neither.

Throughout everything that followed, this remains the most conspicuous irony of all. Vicars' ultimate fate was, in some sense at least, decided by a redundant regulation of his own devising.

2

Hark the Heralds

'That horrid Castle, mother dear,
Thy virtues light its crime exposes,
Yet e'en the dogs while running by,
Put up their paws against their noses.'

From 'Hold Your Noses'
Dublin Weekly News, 1894

Dublin, 1907

DUBLIN, IN THE years after the death of Queen Victoria and the accession of her son Edward VII, was something of an Edwardian outpost – cooler and more accessible than Bombay, but not necessarily more popular among empire builders. It was a provincial city and not especially handsome, even when seen at its best. In addition to its more agreeable features, it included some of the worst slums in Europe.

To many British observers, the Irish were a graceless and insubordinate lot. In 1907, the bulk of the population was, untypically, quiescent but Dublin still had its fair share of political 'agitators'. Most were simply nationalists of one hue or another, people like Arthur Griffith, founder of Sinn Féin, or Maud Gonne, muse of W B Yeats and wife of Boer War guerrilla fighter Major John MacBride. There were one or two persevering socialists but these, generally, 'blushed unseen' in the slums. The heady days of James Larkin and the 1913 Lockout were well in the future.

Despite some earnest attempts at introducing Home Rule on the part of previous Liberal governments, Ireland still returned its elected representatives (mostly members of the moderate Nationalist Party led by John Redmond and John Dillon) to Westminster.

Nowadays, unionism is an exclusively Northern Irish phenomenon but, in 1907, it was dedicated to a United Ireland – albeit a thirty-two county unit loyal to the crown. Southern unionists (those living outside Ulster) had their own newspapers, principally *The Irish Times* and, until 1910, they even had occasional electoral successes. In that year, Major Bryan Cooper was the last unionist to be elected to the House of Commons in an open constituency when he became the MP for South Dublin. Trinity College Dublin, whose electorate was largely uncontaminated by nationalists, continued to return unionists (including Edward Carson) until independence.

The most visible representative of the British monarchy in Ireland was the Lord Lieutenant (also known as the Viceroy). In 1905, at the age of 58, the Liberal peer John Campbell Gordon, Lord Aberdeen, became the incumbent once again, having already held the post for a brief period in 1886. Aberdeen was a kindly, gregarious individual who tended to bend to the will of his over-powering wife, Ishbel Maria. He liked Dublin and the Irish and wanted to be liked in turn. Both he, and his wife, enjoyed the social life of the city and they did not allow themselves to become prisoners of the Viceregal Lodge in the Phoenix Park, either through aloofness or paranoia.

Unionists might have wished that they had. The Aberdeens went out of their way to demonstrate their sympathy with Irish nationalism. Largely as a result of their nationalist inclinations, stories began to proliferate in the unionist press about their stereotypical Scottish meanness. According to vicious Dublin gossip, they fed their guests on 'artificial' jelly and stuffed their roast chickens with plaster, accusations that almost reduced the sensitive Aberdeen to tears. The sniping from *The Irish Times* was particularly fierce.

The role of the Lord Lieutenant was largely symbolic. Real political and administrative power lay with two men: the Chief Secretary for Ireland and the Under Secretary. The former was either an elected MP or a peer and held a cabinet seat, the latter was the leading civil servant in the country. In 1907, these posts were held by the Liberal MP Augustine Birrell and the career public servant Sir Anthony MacDonnell respectively. Birrell was a scholar, minor poet and essayist as well as one of the leading intellectuals of the Liberal administration led by Henry Campbell-Bannerman. As a politician, however, he could be careless and lazy. When he had been asked by his Prime Minister to accept the, often thankless, job of Chief Secretary, he had replied in writing: 'Our conclusion is to do whatever we are bidden. A wise old Tory once gave me this advice. Never ask for anything. Never refuse anything. Never resign anything.' Birrell was not to be allowed to follow the old Tory's final piece of advice. His political career was ruined by the Easter Rising of 1916, for which he was woefully unprepared, and he quit the government in that year.

Most of any Chief Secretary's time was taken up in London, attending cabinet meetings and answering questions in the Commons from some very persistent Irish politicians. So, traditionally, much of the day-to-day running of Irish affairs was left to the Under Secretary. Characteristically, the men who held this post were quiet, rather grey functionaries who shunned the limelight and allowed their political superiors to take responsibility for unpopular actions. Some, however, were tough-minded men who, while not courting publicity, were prepared to take initiatives and risk personal unpopularity. As we shall see later, Sir Anthony MacDonnell fell squarely into this latter category.

Physically, Sir Arthur Vicars was not an impressive man. He was small and thin, with light wispy hair worn parted in the centre and he had a way of looking prim whatever he happened to be doing. His moustache – fussy and expertly curled at both ends – was the only outstanding characteristic of a weak face. It was a face, however, that featured in upwards of two hundred official photographs over a fourteen-year period working in Dublin Castle. Vicars rarely spurned what would be referred to today as a photo opportunity.

Vicars had been born in England in 1864 of Anglo-Irish stock.

His father, Colonel W H Vicars of the 61st Regiment, had died when he was five years old. His mother died five years later. This had been her second marriage, her first had been a wholly Irish affair. She was a Gun-Cunninghame of Wicklow and had married Pierce K Mahony of Kilmorna in County Kerry. They had two children, George and Pierce Mahony. Vicars found himself in the unusual position of being the youngest member of two families and divided his time between them. He was educated in England but spent a large part of each year with his two half-brothers in Ireland.

Vicars developed an interest in genealogy and the obscure science of heraldry early in life. Prolonged academic study of the subject added expertise to mere interest and, from 1890 onwards, he began to canvass the Irish authorities to allow him some way of advancing himself in what was, by then, his chosen profession. On 10th July of that year, he wrote to the Lord Lieutenant's Private Secretary, asking to be appointed to the post of herald or pursuivant (ancient heraldic positions) in the Office of Arms. Two days later, he wrote a similar letter to Arthur Balfour. Balfour, a ruthless and unpopular Tory Chief Secretary known in Ireland as 'Bloody Balfour', was perplexed at the young man's temerity. Vicars enclosed an impressive list of referees, explained that he was a Fellow of the Society of Antiquaries and was the only genealogist in the country who worked outside of the Office of Arms. He even offered to take a post without any pay knowing that, once attached to the Office of Arms, he would be able to develop a healthy private practice. His generous offer was refused.

In 1890, the position of Ulster King of Arms was held by Sir Bernard Burke, who had occupied the post since 1853 and who, by the early-1890s, was an invalid. He was not favourably disposed towards Vicars, recognising in the younger man a threat to his own control of the office and to his desire for the smooth succession of his son Henry. In 1887, he had almost engaged Vicars as his secretary but, when he discovered Vicars' qualifications, he baulked. He offered the excuse that Vicars was too highly qualified for such a tedious position. Vicars was, understandably, peeved. In the course of a letter outlining why he thought he should be given some official role in the Office of Arms, he hinted darkly that Burke was attempting to create a dynasty there.

This first glimpse that we get of Vicars establishes a pattern that will become familiar. He could be almost wilfully tactless and insensitive and was also prone to minor bouts of paranoia, though this was probably justified where Burke was concerned. Burke made quite certain that, despite his undoubted skills, Vicars did not occupy any position whatsoever, paid or otherwise, in the Office of Arms. It is ironic therefore that when Burke died, late in 1892, Vicars quickly got his wish, finally taking up a position in the Office of Arms in 1893. It was a tribute to his expertise and growing reputation that it was not as a junior herald or pursuivant, but as Burke's successor.

At twenty-nine, he was young for the job. But he was a talented genealogist familiar with the heraldic functions he would have to perform. In addition to those duties, Ulster King of Arms – a position created during the Tudor period – was a Knight Attendant on the Order of St Patrick and was also Registrar of the Order and its chief functionary. It was his job to see to the details of investitures and official functions in which the knights might take part. He held his post, under Letters Patent, directly from the King. One year shy of his thirtieth birthday and Vicars had arrived at the pinnacle of the profession of herald in Ireland.

Between 1893 and 1907, Vicars came by a large collection of rare, and consequently expensive, genealogical books. Their acquisition, and the general pursuit of a 'High Tory' lifestyle, caused him a certain amount of financial embarrassment. Enter Francis Richard Shackleton.

Francis Shackleton was Anglo-Irish *haute bourgeoisie* to Vicars' Anglo-Irish patrician. However, even though he was from a well-respected, upper middle-class family, the aura of the *arriviste* still clung to him.

He was born a Quaker, one of the ten children of a gentleman farmer, later a doctor, from County Kildare. Dr Shackleton, yearning to improve himself, had moved to London when Frank was quite young. Among his younger siblings was his brother Ernest, later to become one of the great polar explorers. At first, Frank's interests were quite sedate. He developed a fondness for genealogy and applied for admission, in the late 1890s, to the Herald's College in London, as Vicars had done in his time.

Shackleton sought unpaid work in the Office of Arms in Dublin Castle, in order to gain some valuable experience and enhance his chances of securing admission to the Herald's College. To this end, he wrote to Vicars who agreed to meet him. Vicars was impressed by the extent of the young man's knowledge and displayed a generosity that was typical of him and in marked contrast to his own treatment at the hands of Burke. He offered Shackleton the part-time post of Assistant Secretary to the Office of Arms, a position that Shackleton took up in October 1899. Shackleton also volunteered for the militia (the equivalent of the modern Territorial Army or FCA) and was accepted into the 3rd Battalion, Royal Irish Fusiliers.

In January 1900, his first sojourn in the Office of Arms was ended prematurely by the outbreak of war. He shipped out to South Africa where, unlike a number of his fellow countrymen, he fought *against* the Boers. He was considered a promising soldier and, even though his regiment did not see any action, he was sent out alone on special assignment. After eight months, he was invalided home. He received the Queen's Medal, recuperated from his injuries in Devon and then rejoined his regiment. After the Boer War, he continued his army career for a brief period.

At the request of Vicars, Shackleton made his reappearance in the Office of Arms in 1903 to assist with the arrangements for a state visit by King Edward VII. Shackleton, although no longer holding any official position in the office, was happy to oblige as he was in the process of leaving the army and entering the business world. He was aware that, during the visit, he would be in daily contact with the King – rubbing shoulders with his social 'betters' came quite naturally to him and also enhanced his personal prestige. Advancement came quickly. He had been working with a firm of brokers in the City of London after he h ad left the army and before his brief diversion to Dublin, but soon struck out on his own. He began to put together a series of small business deals all building towards one major coup that, he hoped, would make his fortune. These deals involved speculation in a large tract of Mexican land that was financed through a confusing network of companies and investments. It would later take a court almost a year to disentangle them.

By 1907, Shackleton's world was one of boundless possibility: he had a flat in Park Lane, was a member of at least two fashionable London clubs, was a social success and was considered a budding financial genius. In fact, these last two factors were related. His good looks, education and easy temperament made it simple for him to insinuate himself into the higher echelons of Edwardian society and his business acumen kept him there. He was a useful source of valuable financial information for many aristocrats whose bank balances did not match their pedigrees.

An aspect of his character less widely acknowledged or discussed in his social circle was his homosexuality. It was alleged, at the time, that his return from South Africa had less to do with his injuries than with having been caught *in flagrante* with a fellow soldier. Such an allegation is unverifiable, but there is no doubt about his homosexual nature.

In 1905, when Sir Arthur Vicars revised the Statutes of the Order of St Patrick, he did so, in part, with an eye to the consolidation of his own little empire. He revived three ceremonial posts that year that had been defunct since 1871: Dublin Herald, Cork Herald and Athlone Pursuivant. Fully intending to surround himself with acolytes, the first two appointments he made were straightforward. Shackleton was offered the position of Dublin Herald and Vicars' nephew, Pierce Gun Mahony, that of Cork Herald. With the granting of a position to Shackleton went another proposal: an offer of shared lodgings. Vicars didn't expect Shackleton to make a great commitment of time to the unpaid herald's post, but it was made clear that he would be expected to maintain some sort of residence in the country.

In proposing such an arrangement, Vicars was not being altruistic, he had an ulterior motive. Vicars was conscious of his own financial difficulties. He was not a good manager of money and was having problems meeting the rent on his house in Wellington Road. A co-tenancy agreement with Shackleton would avoid the necessity to move into an unbecomingly smaller dwelling. Shackleton, however, had no need of a residence in Ireland. When he visited Dublin, he stayed with cousins in Terenure and, on the few occasions when the post of herald would actually require him to be in Ireland, he could have continued that practice. He felt, however, that it would have been churlish to refuse as he could afford establishments in both London and Dublin. If he had any reservations about sharing with the rather effete and finicky Vicars, he shrugged them off.

Such was his delight at becoming Dublin Herald that Shackleton made his first patently disadvantageous financial deal. He allowed himself to be talked into an arrangement with Vicars that was little short of outrageous. He agreed to pay half the rent, rates, fuel and servants' wages. He would also pay for half the food consumed when he was in residence, which was not often – in 1907, he stayed in the house for only two weeks.

The two men took up the lease on a semi-detached, early Victorian house in the suburb of Clonskeagh at 7 St James Terrace (now 14 Clonskeagh Road). The arrangement proved very satisfactory. Shackleton was careless of, and Vicars careless with, money.

Both had got what they wanted from the financial deal. On a personal level, the two men became friendly, despite the differences in age and temperament.

The only complaint came from Vicars. He liked to stay up late at night and emerge from his bedroom late the following morning. Shackleton's habits, at least when he was in Dublin, were different. Vicars used to refer to Shackleton as a 'Donegal peasant' because of his habit of getting up early each morning with a jauntiness that irritated the older man. Shackleton was used to London business hours, Vicars was not.

The appointment of his nephew, Pierce Gun Mahony, to the post of Cork Herald, caused Vicars annoyance of a different kind. Mahony was the son of his half-brother, Pierce O'Mahony, a passionate Irish nationalist. But Pierce junior had reacted against his father's brand of nationalism (hinted at by the dropping of the 'O' prefix from his name) and was delighted to accept the post of Cork Herald. The offer of the position coincided nicely with the direction he had chosen for himself. The appointment, however, incensed his father. Vicars, naively, thought that his half-brother would be glad to see the advancement of his son and felt he was repaying some of the care and attention he had received from his two half-brothers in his youth. It never occurred to him that the virulently nationalistic Pierce O'Mahony might be irritated to see his son throw in his lot with the Dublin Castle establishment. The appointment of Pierce Gun Mahony to the Cork Herald post led to an estrangement between the two half-brothers that was to last for two years.

At the time of his appointment in 1905, Mahony was twenty-seven years of age and married to an Englishwoman, Ethel Wright, the daughter of a Yorkshire doctor. His part in the drama of the theft of the jewels is largely peripheral, but his eventual fate was no less tragic than that of the others caught up in the affair.

The final ceremonial post revived by Vicars was that of Athlone Pursuivant. Sometime in 1905, when he was redrawing the Statutes of the Order, Vicars had been introduced to Francis Bennett Goldney who, at forty-nine years of age, was an aspiring politician in the southern English city of Canterbury. He had been elected mayor of the city in the teeth of Liberal opposition and the antipathy of elements within his own local Conservative Party. He was also, like Vicars, a Fellow of the Royal Society of Antiquaries.

Goldney's family name was Evans but, in 1892, he had come into an unusual inheritance. In order to benefit from it, he was obliged to assume his mother's maiden name, Bennett Goldney. The bequest had been used wisely and he became a magpie collector, buying *objets d'art* of all kinds. Goldney hoped to parlay his antiquarian expertise into a prestigious sinecure that would advance his political career. After a determined lobbying campaign, he was appointed to the vacant position of Athlone Pursuivant in February 1907, although he had no connection whatsoever with Ireland.

To this day, the Bedford Tower is one of the outstanding architectural features of the Upper Yard in Dublin Castle. Its exterior has not changed greatly but, since its transformation in the 1990s into a Conference Centre, its interior has altered quite radically. In 1907, you would have walked through the front door of the tower into a circular foyer. Straight ahead was the office used by the messenger with a connecting door to the strong-room. On the right was the door to the library that housed the safe containing the Crown Jewels and some of the collars of the Knights of the Order of St Patrick. As you entered the library, you might easily have missed the safe, partly obscured as it was by a long table running down the centre of the room.

As well as being a repository for most of the books in the office, the library was used as a waiting room. People would frequently call to see one or other of the heralds, each of whom had their own private practice – the heralds compensated for the unpaid nature of their official positions by accepting fees for undertaking genealogical searches for members of the public anxious to trace their ancestry.

When a visitor came to see one of the heralds he, or she, would be shown into the library by William Stivey, a retired sailor, who was the Office of Arms messenger. When a visitor asked to see one of the officials, Stivey would ring upstairs on the internal phone. Occasionally, some of the officials would work in the library, particularly on complex searches, as most of the books they would need were close at hand. Much of Vicars' costly manuscript collection was stored in glass cases in the strong-room, which also contained a number of other objects of intrinsic and symbolic value. There was, for example, the Sword of State, which would be ceremonially handed over from one Lord Lieutenant to another to mark the beginning of a new Viceroyalty. Also stored there were two maces, as well as the sceptre and coronet of Ulster King of Arms.

By 21st-century standards, Vicars had a somewhat relaxed attitude towards security. The position of the Office of Arms, within the confines of the nerve centre of police activity in Ireland, seems to have engendered a certain complacency when it came to any concern about the safety of the jewels or other regalia. Vicars frequently displayed the jewels to any visitors he wished to impress. This was particularly the case where female guests were concerned, as they tended to be more appreciative.

Vicars himself worked in an office that suited his pretensions on the first floor of the Bedford Tower. It was spacious and well appointed with dark wooden panelling around the walls and two windows facing out onto the Upper Castle Yard. In between the windows was a door that opened onto a balcony with two large circular stone columns. Adjoining Vicars' room was that of the Office of Arms Secretary, George Dames Burtchaell. Sharp, intelligent and decisive, Burtchaell was a true professional among gentlemen and amateurs. In terms of genealogical expertise, he was surpassed only by Vicars, though he easily excelled his superior when it came to administrative ability.

On the second floor were the offices of Sydney Horlock, Vicars' Personal Secretary and Mary Gibbon, the highly efficient office typist. In January 1907, Vicars had been staying in London, had seen an advertisement, placed by Horlock, in a London newspaper and had interviewed him. Vicars was impressed enough to offer him a job and Horlock was anxious enough for employment to accept. He had moved to Ireland within a matter of days and had spent a while with Vicars in Clonskeagh before he found lodgings for himself.

The only other employee of the Office of Arms was Mrs Mary Farrell, the office cleaner. She was a widow whose husband had died in 1895 leaving her with four sons. One had subsequently died in an accident and, in order to make a living, she had been forced to allow the other three to be housed in an orphanage. But, by 1907, she had been reunited with her children in a modest flat in the Iveagh Buildings around the corner from Dublin Castle. Each of her boys, though all now employed themselves, were expected to help out in the domestic chores associated with the Office of Arms.

That, in July 1907, was Vicars' small complement of regular and occasional genealogists, office workers and cleaning staff. None would remain untouched by the events that were about to unfold. Events, far more dramatic than anything the Bedford Tower had ever previously witnessed.

3

The Theft

WEDNESDAY, 3RD JULY should not have been an exceptional day
for Mrs Mary Farrell. She arrived at the Office of Arms shortly
before eight o'clock, as she did every day during the summer.
Having passed the patrolling sentries, she reached the Bedford
Tower and took out her latchkey to open the front door (the door
also had a mortise lock, but this was never used). As Mrs Farrell
pushed her key into the latch, the door swung open. Surprised,
she examined the lock closely. The catch was back.

She entered the building warily. The catch could have been
left on from the previous night by accident or one of the office
staff might have decided to start work bright and early – though
neither had ever happened before. A cautious search revealed
that the building was empty. For the moment, Mrs Farrell dismissed the matter from her mind and set about her duties.

The times at which those associated with the Office of Arms
began their working day bore an inverse relationship to the insti-
tutional pecking order. The office cleaner was always in first,

hours before anybody else. Normally, she would have left, pulling the door after herself, before Stivey, the office messenger, arrived and let himself in. Mrs Farrell would have finished by ten o'clock on most mornings, depending on what tasks she had set herself.

Stivey's day began between ten and ten thirty. After him, the remainder of the retinue would begin to trickle in. Horlock, Vicars' Private Secretary, and Mary Gibbon, the typist, would arrive shortly after Stivey, followed by the office secretary, George Burtchaell. Sir Arthur Vicars, as befitted a man of his consequence, would rarely be seen before eleven. The heralds and pursuivants were only expected to attend infrequently as their posts were voluntary and unpaid. Pierce Gun Mahony was the most conscientious, but even he was absent for long periods. Francis Shackleton attended intermittently; Francis Bennett Goldney hardly at all.

Although Mrs Farrell had finished her morning's work by ten, she decided to wait on that morning of 3rd July. She wanted to pass on the information about the unlocked door, however inconsequential it might be. She didn't have to wait long before Stivey arrived. Promising to relay her story to Vicars, Stivey tried, when she left, to remember the previous night. Had he been the last to leave? Might he have forgotten to release the catch? The door of the Office of Arms was left unlocked all day and normally Sir Arthur Vicars would be the last to depart, so he would slip the latch. But perhaps, thought Stivey, he had been last out himself on that Tuesday evening.

Then he remembered, with some relief, that Owen Kerr, a Dublin Metropolitan Police detective, always did his tour around the building at about seven o'clock every night, after everyone had gone home. If anyone had forgotten to lock the door, he reflected, it would have been Kerr. The messenger was sitting at his desk, in his alcove beside the strong-room, when he heard the customary rumpus that greeted Vicars' arrival, amid the usual flurry of despatch boxes and files. Stivey went out to greet him and relieve him of some of the boxes.

As Sir Arthur ascended the winding staircase to his first-floor office, the messenger was instructed to follow him. At his desk, Vicars began, straightaway, to busy himself separating various letters and documents. Stivey waited for an appropriate moment. As his employer didn't seem to have noticed his continued presence, he broke the silence. 'Sir Arthur, earlier on, when I came in, Mrs Farrell was waiting for me. She told me that, when she went to let herself into the office this morning, she found the door unlocked.'

The messenger paused to allow the significance of this information to sink in. Vicars looked up impassively. 'Did she?' he asked, absently.

Stivey continued to wait. He had been preparing his answer to the inevitable question: had he left the door unlocked the night before? However, Sir Arthur continued to sort out his papers, appearing to be blissfully unconcerned. It was as if Stivey had never spoken, as if he was no longer there. Puzzled by this total lack of interest in what he had considered to be weighty information, the messenger withdrew from the office and went about his business.

On 10th July 1907, Edward VII was to begin a brief visit to Dublin. It was the King's intention to tour the Irish International

Exhibition, the national industrial showpiece that had been opened by Lord Aberdeen on 4th May. While in Dublin, he would also assist at the investiture of Lord Castletown as a Knight of St Patrick and, combining business with pleasure, would attend the Leopardstown Races. He would be accompanied by a party of twenty and Lord Aberdeen, ever the parsimonious Lord Lieutenant, nearly had apoplexy when informed of the numbers he would be expected to entertain in the Viceregal Lodge.

Aberdeen decided that he and his wife could not possibly cope with such an entourage and would have to pass up the privilege of accommodating the King. It was arranged that the King would sleep on board his own yacht (and at his own expense) in Kingstown (Dún Laoghaire) Harbour. By way of excusing what might be taken as a severe discourtesy, Aberdeen pointed out that the 'drive of ten miles to the city each day [would give] a splendid opportunity for the manifestation of cordial welcome and goodwill on the part of the population'.

It was left to Sir Arthur Vicars to supervise many of the arrangements for the King's visit. He was already responsible for the arrangements surrounding the investiture of Lord Castletown and, by the beginning of July, was starting to feel the pressure of the extra work allocated to him. Such was his growing obsession with the finer details of the approaching event that, when Stivey passed on the information about the front door on the morning of Wednesday 3rd July, no warning bells sounded.

On Friday 5th July, Vicars and Horlock finished work at about ten minutes past seven. The Bedford Tower was deserted as they made ready to leave. When they got to the bottom of the stairs, Vicars turned to Horlock and said, 'Wait until I make my usual tour of inspection.' He then walked into the library, checked all the doors of the bookcases, passed into Stivey's room, checked the window at the back and tested the handle of the strong-room door. He then rejoined Horlock and both men left the building, locking the door behind them. Vicars drove to the Kildare Street Club, stayed for about a quarter of an hour and then left for home. He was back in Clonskeagh by eight o'clock.

The following day all hell broke loose around him.

Early on Saturday morning, 6th July, Mrs Farrell arrived for work. She let herself in with her latchkey, as usual, and went straight over to Stivey's desk to check for any notes from Sir Arthur or any other member of the staff. There was no note today. But, as she turned to leave the room, Mrs Farrell saw something else that greatly alarmed her, something that had never happened since the move to the Bedford Tower. The door of the strong-room was ajar. The gap was wide enough to allow anyone to pass in or out comfortably. Although the office was quiet, it occurred to her that there might be someone inside.

She waited and listened but still there wasn't a sound. Finally, she looked through the opening. The grille inside was locked and the key was in place, from it hung a smaller key that opened the presses in the strong-room. What was she to do? She had no key of her own to lock the strong-room door but she couldn't just leave the door half open with the grille key nestling invitingly in its lock. She made her decision quickly. Taking the keys from the grille lock, she banged the door shut. After she'd finished her cleaning, she settled in to wait for Stivey just as she'd done three mornings previously. But it was Saturday and the messenger was taking advantage of the fact that his masters were even tardier on Saturdays than weekdays. Eventually, she tired of waiting and, spotting a blotting pad on Stivey's desk, scribbled out a note: 'Mr Stivey, I found the strong-room door open this morning. I have closed it and I closed the gate and leave the keys on your table.' With that, she left.

At about twenty minutes past ten, Stivey arrived. His attention was immediately drawn to the set of keys on the table in his room. He read Mrs Farrell's note. The two keys he held in his hand were mute witnesses to the fact that someone had tampered with the strong-room door. Stivey distinctly remembered having locked the door the previous night, having first checked with Vicars that the books in the strong-room were no longer needed. He went straight to the room and quickly surveyed its contents. Everything was as it should have been. Nothing had been touched. For the second time that week, Stivey waited anxiously for Sir Arthur Vicars to arrive.

At eleven, a package was delivered from the jewellers West's of Grafton Street containing the gold collar that had belonged to the late Lord de Ros. De Ros had been a Knight of St Patrick for a few years prior to his death and Vicars had made representations to his widow, as the 1905 Statutes of the Order obliged him to do, to return the collar. It had been sent from London directly to West's to be cleaned and have Lord de Ros' name engraved on it. The box was left on Sir Arthur's desk for his inspection.

Vicars reached the Office of Arms between eleven thirty and midday and Stivey followed him up the stairs. Vicars' room was rather crowded when they arrived. Mahony was already at work as were Horlock and Miss Gibbon. Stivey decided to choose his moment before telling Vicars of Mrs Farrell's note. His decision was probably prompted by natural discretion and a desire to let Vicars hear the news and handle the affair in private. Also, after the previous Wednesday, he must have felt he needed the undivided attention of his superior.

His chance came at about one o'clock when Vicars ventured downstairs to make a call from the office telephone in Stivey's room. When he had finished, the messenger approached him. 'Sir Arthur, when I arrived in the office this morning, I found a note on my table from Mrs Farrell telling me she had found the strong-room open. She closed it and left the grille key for me.'

Once again Stivey waited. He waited for Vicars to enter the strong-room and make a thorough search. He expected, at the very least, to be asked had he done so himself. Instead Vicars looked at him absentmindedly. 'Is that so?' he asked, and walked past Stivey up the stairs to his office.

Stivey was taken aback at Vicars' nonchalance. Whatever about the front door, surely the fact that the strong-room had been found open deserved a less dismissive response? Stivey was, however, a naval man. He was conscious of chains of command, of what happens to subordinates who take unwelcome and unnecessary initiatives. Any anxiety he might have felt for the safety of the jewels, he kept to himself. At two fifteen, Stivey decided his day's work was done, it was his long-established custom to leave early on Saturdays. Even though the other officials seemed to be scurrying about, fussing over the royal visit, Stivey reasoned that King Edward's trip would be no less comfortable or memorable if the Office of Arms messenger decided to take the rest of Saturday off.

He liked to be circumspect about these things and so he made another trip upstairs to the overpopulated office. He would never simply ask to be allowed to leave, it was more a case of, 'Will that be all for today, Sir?' Before the messenger had time to put the question to Vicars, who had been conversing with Mahony, Sir Arthur rose from his desk and handed him the box that had arrived that morning from West's. 'I wish you would take this collar and put it down in the safe,' said Vicars, reaching into his pocket. 'We are getting overcrowded here. We are getting congested.' Stivey later recalled that Vicars produced a bunch of keys from his pocket, indicated the key of the safe and handed the bunch to the messenger.

Stivey was astonished. His hierarchical sensibilities rebelled. Imbued as he was with respect for rank, he was also aware of the accepted limits of delegation. On board ship, there were certain functions that were the captain's and the captain's alone and which he did not depute ordinary seamen to perform. Vicars had hardly ever been known to part with the key to the safe. He had certainly never handed it to Stivey before. But the old sailor's background and training had not accustomed him to 'reason why'. He might have been puzzled by Vicar's behaviour, but he dutifully accepted the key. He didn't even point out to his superior that he had only the scantest idea of how to open the safe.

Vicars resumed his conversation with Mahony and Stivey left the room. He arrived at the safe and placed the collar box on top of it. The lock was similar to the one to the door of the strong-room: two keyholes faced him. He tried the lower one first. The key didn't move. It occurred to him that the mechanism might be exactly the reverse of the one to which he was more accustomed. He inserted the key in the upper lock. This time it moved. He tried the handle but it wouldn't budge. He realised that he had locked the safe.

After a lifetime spent at sea, Stivey was no stranger to drama, but all this was a little too much for him. Never before had he been asked to open the safe. Now, when the responsibility had been thrust upon him, he found the safe already open. Gathering his wits, he took the key from the lock, grabbed the collar box and started back up the stairs. This time they would have to listen to him. As he moved towards the library door, he heard footsteps leaving the room overhead. By the time Stivey had got to the bottom of the stairs, Vicars had already reached the landing and was on his way down. Stivey was relieved, clearly common sense had prevailed and he was coming to supervise the operation. The two men met halfway.

'Sir Arthur,' exclaimed the unnerved messenger, 'the last time you were at the safe you could not have locked the door.'

'Oh!' replied Vicars. 'I must have done.'

'Well, I found the safe door unlocked.'

'What do you mean?' enquired the puzzled Vicars.

Vicars was galvanised. He moved rapidly into the library, taking the keys from Stivey as he went and opened the safe. At first glance, everything seemed intact. Then he spotted a key in the lock of the box that contained the Grand Master's Insignia, the Crown Jewels. It was a key that he usually left hidden in one of the other boxes. Stivey heard him mutter, 'The key is in the lock. I wonder if they are all right?' Vicars knelt down and, nervously, opened the box. Empty! He stared at it for a moment, paralysed. Shaking off his inertia he shouted, 'My God, they are gone. The jewels are gone!'

Vicars realised then that the situation might be even worse, because he quickly snatched up one of the five collar boxes and flipped open the lid. All that remained was the wrapping paper. He opened the other four boxes in turn, all with the same result. He scanned the safe again. Something else was missing. He had left his mother's jewels locked in a box in the safe. Rather than attempt to open it on the spot, the thieves had simply removed the box. He made one last desultory survey of the contents of the safe but only found the patent under which he held his office. A man with a dark sense of humour might have been forgiven an ironic laugh at this untimely reminder of his responsibilities. He opened the box that had contained the Crown Jewels as if hoping to conjure them back. It was then that he noticed something that had escaped his attention at first. The box was not completely empty. The ribbon and the clasp that had fastened the Badge to the ceremonial garments of the Lord Lieutenant had been left behind.

More surprising was the fact that the ribbon had not been cut or damaged in any way. The Badge had been connected to the ribbon by two small screws that would have required a few precious minutes to undo. It would have been far simpler to have taken the lot or done a neat job with a pair of scissors. This last reproving vestige of the regalia punctured the aura of disbelief that briefly protected Vicars from reality. He had been responsible for the Crown Jewels and they had vanished, stolen from under his eyes. Vicars had two options. As realisation dawned, he could calmly allow his native intelligence and rationality to reassert itself or he could succumb to blind panic and do all the wrong things. He chose the line of least resistance and panicked!

Had he kept his head, he might have remembered what Stivey had told him that morning and quizzed the messenger about the strong-room. He might have made a close inspection of the contents of that room to see if any more of the insignia had vanished. Much of the remaining insignia was too bulky or awkward to carry, but there were some gold collars that had been prominently displayed. He might also have sent immediately for some working detectives – instead, he went straight to the top. The first thing he instructed Stivey to do was to fetch Sir John Ross, the Commissioner of the Dublin Metropolitan Police and M V Harrel, the Assistant Commissioner. After Stivey had left, Vicars went upstairs to break the news to Mahony and Burtchaell. The secretary was just getting ready to leave when, as he later recalled, Vicars burst in. 'Burtchaell,' he exclaimed, 'a dreadful thing has happened.'

The first thing that crossed Burtchaell's mind was that, after all their preparations, something had occurred to cancel the King's visit. Little else could account for Vicars' obvious agitation. 'The safe has been opened,' Sir Arthur blurted out, 'and the badges and jewels have been taken!'

'When did you discover this?' asked an incredulous Burtchaell.

'Just now! Can you remember when the safe was opened last?'

Burtchaell could not. 'Of course,' he asked, 'you have told the police?' When his superior mentioned the imminent arrival of Ross and Harrel, Burtchaell advised Vicars, 'You ought to send to the Detective Office at once,' he advised. 'The sooner this is known to the police the better.'

Finally, Vicars took the point and a message was sent to the Detective Office. Burtchaell and he then walked downstairs to survey the damage together. While waiting for the arrival of the DMP, Burtchaell looked for signs of forcible entry. A cursory inspection undertaken after a reference by Vicars to 'burglars' revealed nothing. In addition, Vicars had mentioned that '*he* [the burglar] was at the strong-room also'. Burtchaell thought nothing of this remark at the time. He assumed that the door had been tampered with but that nothing had been taken. It is plain, however, that Vicars' memory of the information conveyed earlier that day by Stivey was beginning to stir.

At about this time, Assistant Commissioner Harrel arrived. He was closely followed by Superintendent Lowe of the Detective Office. Vicars went over his story once again and concluded by introducing his first scapegoat. He told Harrel, 'This is the fault of the Board of Works, I asked them for a safe in the strong-room and they did not give it; if they had given it this would not have happened. I have the correspondence upstairs, and will show it to you.'

At this stage, probably less than enthralled by the bureaucratic trend the conversation was taking, Lowe intervened. He asked Vicars if he could see the box that had contained the jewels. Vicars handed him the red morocco case and drew his attention to the ribbon and the clasp left inside. Lowe assumed that the ribbon had already been detached from the Badge and, when he was told otherwise, his curiosity was immediately aroused. Vicars explained to him how the ribbon had been attached with two screws and demonstrated how difficult they were to manipulate and how long it would have taken to coax the ribbon from its hook on the Badge.

Lowe then began to question Vicars about the keys to the safe. He was told that there were two: the one that had been handed to Stivey and a spare that Vicars kept at home, safely concealed in his desk. Vicars next began to cast doubts on the safe. It was a Ratner model, made by Ratcliffe and Horner and Vicars suddenly decided that, all along, he had been unsure of its effectiveness. The lock on the strong-room door, for example, was a Milner, and he had 'implicit confidence in it'. Vicars' remark alerted Lowe to the fact that there were more valuables in the strong-room. When asked had the door been tampered with, Vicars said, 'No!'

It was the lie direct. Only minutes before, Vicars had indicated to Burtchaell, without elaborating, that something had happened to the strong-room. When Lowe asked him the question, it must have caused Vicars a moment of sublime consternation. This query would lead to others that, in turn, would lead to the inescapable conclusion that he had been negligent in ignoring Stivey. In the short term, it was far simpler to lie. Stivey was present when the question was posed – he had been opening and closing the front door as people arrived and left – and heard Vicars commit his faux pas. He was bewildered and perplexed, but he did not contradict his chief. He thereby helped seal his own fate. (It was not until the following day that the police heard about the strong-room door from the estimable Mrs Farrell.)

Satisfied with the response to his question, Lowe began examining the safe. Harrel intervened to ask when Vicars had last seen the jewels.

'I believe I showed them to Mr Hodgson,' replied Vicars distractedly, referring to his friend and fellow antiquarian, J C

Hodgson, librarian to the Duke of Northumberland.

'When?' asked Lowe.

'I'm not sure,' admitted Vicars. 'But,' he added quickly, 'we've got the visitors book.' The two men checked the entries. Hodgson had visited the office on 11th June.

Harrel insisted that Hodgson be wired immediately and asked if he had been shown the jewels. 'But that would let everyone know about it,' protested Vicars.

Harrel concealed his irritation. 'That does not necessarily follow, but it must be done.'

Vicars was starting to flounder, but he continued to demur. Burtchaell, who had witnessed Harrel's mounting annoyance, now intervened. 'Why don't you do what Mr Harrel tells you?'

'What can I say?' Vicars enquired of Harrel.

Harrel contained his exasperation. Writing material was sent for and he dictated: 'Am anxious to know latest date on which safe with jewels was opened. Do you recollect whether I showed them to you when here?'

At four o'clock, DMP Commissioner Sir John Ross arrived. He made no practical contribution. He added nothing to the sum of anyone's knowledge. He simply lent a tone to the proceedings that they scarcely required. Vicars went over his story again. Ross rediscovered the ribbon in the red morocco case and the paper in the collar boxes and made apposite observations.

Amid all that rank and stature, Owen Kerr must have looked oddly misplaced and felt it too. However, there was slightly more purpose to Kerr's presence than that of the more exalted policemen. He was the officer who made the tour of inspection every night and, while he doesn't come across as the brightest of detectives, at least he had some local knowledge. He had no sooner arrived than Vicars began to spread the burden of culpability even more thinly.

'Kerr,' he said, 'the jewels are all gone; some of the smart boys that have been over for the King's visit made a clean sweep of them.' The ritual condemnation of the Board of Works followed and, for the umpteenth time that day, Vicars related how the theft had been discovered.

Now Stivey suddenly came to life. Why he should choose to do so at this point rather than when Vicars had emphatically denied that the strong-room had been tampered with, is anybody's guess. Perhaps, he was watching the blame being none too skilfully laid off by Vicars and wondered how long it would be before some adhered to himself. More probably, he felt it was time to make his contribution now that a responsible party had arrived with whom he was more familiar and more comfortable. He told the assembled crowd about having found the safe door unlocked.

'Though I am here six years,' he told Kerr, 'I never had that key in my hand before.'

Vicars moved to retrieve the situation. 'Yes,' he agreed, 'that is so. I was thronged owing to pressure of business and I sent Stivey, but I was coming immediately after him.'

Harrel and Ross left shortly after this and Lowe then began an intensive two-hour interrogation of Vicars. While this was in progress, a reply came from Hodgson to the wire. He had seen the jewels. That established 11th June as the last time the Crown Jewels had been seen, intact and *in situ*. The questioning by Lowe was thorough, but still the issue of Mrs Farrell's discovery that morning did not arise.

After Lowe left, Vicars was calmer than at any time since the theft had been discovered and he was able to dash off a letter to Hodgson in time to catch the post. In spite of his previously expressed fears that wiring his acquaintance was tantamount to publicising the fact of the robbery, he told Hodgson everything, adding that: 'The police are hard at it and the hue and cry will be raised all over Europe, but for the present please keep this to yourself absolutely – it is awkward for me, but what more can a mortal do when a safe lock is picked as appears to be the case, for no sign of tampering with safe or lock is visible.'

Assistant Commissioner Harrel returned at about five o'clock and asked Vicars to show him the strong-room and its contents. He began enquiring about keys again. Who had keys to what door? How many were there of each? Vicars became defensive. He produced his key ring and showed Harrel how he kept both the key of the strong-room and the key of the safe on his chain. Harrel was dubious.

'Now, is that really the case?' he enquired.

'Yes it is,' Vicars insisted. 'They have never left my possession; I have always been most careful.'

What Vicars told Harrel was true, as far as it went. He was not in the habit of handing over his safe key to anyone. What he neglected to mention was that, although he possessed the only two keys to the safe, there had been no less than four strong-room keys in circulation as well as seven latchkeys for the front door.

For obvious reasons, Harrel's more immediate concern was the safe. He asked Vicars if there was another key. Vicars told him about the spare, concealed in his secretaire at home. Surprised to learn that this had not been sent for already, Harrel asked Vicars to go immediately and confirm that the key was secure. Vicars, however, was beginning to recover his magisterial aplomb. He coolly told Harrel that he was too busy to go and look for the key. He would be leaving the office at about seven that evening and would see to it then. Harrel instructed Vicars to phone him as soon as he had located the key.

Almost as an afterthought, Harrel asked Vicars if he had any suggestions to offer as to who might have committed the crime. Too often that afternoon Vicars had spoken thoughtlessly. He was used to speaking to the likes of Harrel socially but had not had dealings with him on a professional level before. It seemed to escape his attention that his remarks were being carefully noted, would at some stage be repeated and might conceivably be acted upon. He would have done well to think before he spoke, but he didn't. In response to Harrel's question he singled out as a suspect his own coachman, Phillips.

It was, in many ways, a convenient choice. Phillips had access to his employer's keys. In fact, on one occasion, he had even brought them from Clonskeagh to the Castle when they had been left behind. But Phillips' best qualification as a suspect was probably that, unlike others who might have fitted the bill equally well, he was not a 'gentleman'. Vicars' was, generally, a thoughtful and decent man, but his shabby treatment of Phillips reflected little credit upon him. He could have been desperately seeking to protect himself or he might have irresponsibly thought aloud to Harrel. Either way, the police took him seriously and Phillips was turned inside out by the subsequent investigation. To add to Phillilps' woes, Vicars dismissed him.

Much later, when the police were satisfied that Phillips had had nothing whatsoever to do with the robbery, Vicars was remorseful. Phillips had no desire to take up his employment again but, justifiably, felt entitled to some reparation. Vicars redeemed himself somewhat by paying passage for Phillips, his wife and their four children to the United States.

When he finally returned home that night, Sir Arthur did as Harrel had instructed. He found the spare key of the safe as he had left it and contacted Harrel immediately. He also sent off a telegram to his friend Francis Bennett Goldney that read simply: 'Come at once.'

Sometime that evening, Vicars had a visit from his nephew Pierce Gun Mahony but his relative had come neither to gossip nor commiserate. During the day, Mahony had been party to some of the events unfolding in the Office of Arms. When he returned to his house in Burlington Road that night, he went straight to his desk. There he found his key to the front door of the Bedford Tower, as well as a key of the strong-room. He had called round to his uncle in Clonskeagh to dispose of both keys as quickly as if they were the jewels themselves.

Before he retired that night, Vicars sat down to write yet another letter to his friend Hodgson. There was now a bond between these two men. They were the last bona fide antiquaries to see the Irish Crown Jewels intact. Given what he had said about the Ratner safe to the police, Vicars' letter is revealing: 'The safe is a fine one, Ratcliffe and Horner, and the key of it never left my possession. It was always a source of anxiety to me, having charge of things of such value and, during the Castle season, I had to take them to the Lord Lieutenant on full dress nights, and again get them up and lock them up in the safe, often at 3.00 am, but the police were always about, and a detective patrolled through my office at night. The safe, as you know, was just inside a window, outside which a sentry patrolled night and day and the guard room of the Castle was next to my office. The lock must have been picked or else a duplicate key got.'

It is not recorded whether Sir Arthur Vicars slept soundly on the night of 6th July.

4

Raising Kane

ON THE SEVENTH day, nobody rested.

Detective Owen Kerr was having a busy day. Sir Arthur Vicars may have conveyed the impression in his letter to Hodgson of a vigilant guard dog with a finely honed sense of danger ceaselessly stalking the Office of Arms ready to pounce at anything that moved without authorisation – but Kerr was more Dachshund than Doberman. He was a decent hard-working police officer but had, over the years, been dulled somewhat by the routine of his job.

He made his inspection of the Castle offices every night of the week. His itinerary never varied. He would search the State Apartments shortly after five thirty and would reach the Office of Arms about an hour later. His timing might vary on occasions, but only slightly.

Kerr had only a dim awareness of what exactly it was that he was protecting in the course of his evening inspection. He had some small notion that the safe he saw every night in the corner of the Office of Arms contained some gold collars, but he was unaware of the existence of the Badge and Star. That was until 7th July, when he found out all about the Crown Jewels. As the police-man most directly involved in the safeguarding of the jewels, he must have wondered what scenarios were going through the minds of his superiors. At some stage, they would be called upon to apportion blame. What would his portion be?

On that Sunday afternoon, Kerr visited the home of Mrs Mary Farrell in the nearby Iveagh Buildings. He wasn't expecting much, the office cleaner was, apparently, peripheral to the drama. He felt she was unlikely to be able to add anything to what he already knew. So Kerr must have found it difficult to believe her story. He had spent a couple of hours in the Office of Arms on Saturday afternoon and, at no stage, had anybody mentioned the salient fact that the strong-room door had been found open ear-lier that morning. Neither had Sir Arthur thought to tell him that Mrs Farrell had discovered the front door open the previous Wednesday.

But it was another piece of information volunteered by the office cleaner that nonplussed Kerr completely. These were the facts as she related them to the detective.

Some months earlier, in February or March of 1907, at about ten o'clock, she had been upstairs when she had heard the front door of the tower open. She came downstairs to investigate. The door of the library was open and, when she entered, a man was standing in front of her. The intruder had clearly not expected company. Obviously confused, he muttered something like, 'It is all right', made as if to leave a note on the long table in the centre of the library and then left.

Curious, Mrs Farrell went over to the table where the man had seemed to be writing. There was nothing there. She walked over to the front door. It was just as she had left it, closed and locked. There was no sign that the door had been forced in any way. It dawned on her that the mysterious visitor had been able to let himself in. He had had his own latchkey. She had waited to break the news to Stivey, but that was the last she had heard of the incident. There had been no follow-up inquiry of any kind despite the presence of an intruder in the Bedford Tower. Mrs Farrell knew that the visitor was unconnected with the Office of Arms and, though not absolutely certain, she thought she had recognised him. The policeman enquired who she thought it was. 'Haddo,' she replied.

The information startled Kerr, as it did others when it was passed on. Lord Haddo was the son of the Lord Lieutenant, Lord Aberdeen. He had no business whatsoever in the Office of Arms, least of all before it opened for the day. He had also no entitlement whatsoever to any means of access to the office. Kerr must have foreseen trouble on the horizon when he reported Mrs Farrell's statement to his superiors.

Mrs Farrell was not as much on the margins of affairs as Kerr might have originally believed. She was familiar with most of the leading Castle functionaries, particularly those connected with the Office of Arms. As he was extremely friendly with Vicars and Shackleton, she knew Haddo well – well enough to have cultivated an intense dislike of the man. Her children were familiar with her way of designating disapproval. To her, Vicars was always 'Sir Arthur', Frank Shackleton was always 'Mr Shackleton', while George, Lord Haddo (afterwards the 2nd Marquess of Aberdeen and Temair) was just plain 'Haddo'.

However, Mrs Farrell told Kerr that she would be reluctant to identify Haddo publicly or in open court, as she was not absolutely positive that he was the man she had seen. Having been told of the theft of the jewels, she realised the significance of her information. She would not blacken a man's reputation (even that of a person she disliked) on the basis of what she thought she had seen that morning. Others were less reluctant.

Kerr was quick to pass all of this startling new information on to his superiors. The misgivings of the professionally suspicious Superintendent Lowe must have increased. Vicars had been asked directly if the strong-room had been tampered with. Why had he wilfully held back information? The police began to wonder about Vicars and checked his movements minutely. His account of his activities tallied with that of alibi witnesses. Their suspicions about Vicars abated.

The police did, however, uncover something interesting in their scrutiny of Vicars' movements. They didn't consider it significant, but it was. All those who had been on guard duty at the various gates that night were closely questioned. None were able to say at what time Vicars had left the Castle. It was his habit to enter by the Ship Street Gate and leave via the Main Gate, but nobody could say positively that they had noticed him leave. Vicars would have been a familiar sight to the sentries. His comings and goings were unthreatening and routine. Why should they have particularly noted his exit on one night that, to all intents and purposes, was like any other? Extend this further and it begs an important question: how many of those associated with the Office of Arms, or the many other Castle institutions, became similarly inconspicuous by virtue of their familiarity?

While Vicars was being investigated by the DMP, three men were making their separate preparations to travel to Dublin from England: two were making the journey for similar reasons, the third had a very different purpose.

When Francis Bennett Goldney received Sir Arthur Vicars' telegram, telling him to 'come at once', he was already in the throes of his preparations for the journey. Goldney was due to make his second public appearance as Athlone Pursuivant. He had already attended the opening ceremony for the International Exhibition in Ballsbridge. His second engagement would be given an added piquancy by the attendance of the King. Such proximity to his sovereign was unlikely to do the career of the would-be Conservative MP the slightest harm.

His intention had been to arrive in Dublin shortly before the King's visit but, when he had received Vicars' telegram, he quickly changed his plans and got a boat on the night of 7th July. Perhaps he did so out of disinterested friendship. On the other hand, he knew that Vicars had been unwell, he may have wanted to be on hand in case Vicars was forced to redistribute his functions for the royal visit. He might edge closer to the King and so inch closer to Westminster.

Goldney disembarked from the mail boat at seven o'clock on the morning of Monday 8th, in wretched condition. The crossing had been a rough one. Thoughts of exchanging cordial and profitable pleasantries with the King were far from his mind as he drove from Kingstown to Clonskeagh. Of primary importance were a bath and some breakfast. He was totally unprepared for the news that had prompted Vicars to send the telegram.

'Have you heard the awful news?' Vicars asked as soon as Goldney arrived.

All Goldney had on his mind was the awful crossing and the retching of his fellow passengers. 'No!' he replied.

Vicars quickly filled him in. He expected Goldney to be shocked at his vicissitudes and his friend did not disappoint. Having expressed the required amount of indignation, Goldney was allowed to wash and eat. Later, whatever shock he might have felt didn't prevent him from getting a few hours rest and dashing off a couple of letters.

Frank Shackleton was returning to Ireland for the same reason as Goldney. He had left Dublin on the 7th or 8th June after a garden party thrown by Lady Ardilaun. While in England, most of his time was spent in London in his flat in Park Lane.

Shackleton was just beginning to enjoy the fruits of his shrewdness as a businessman. He could afford the upkeep of his flat, a house in Devon and a half-share in the house in Clonskeagh. He gave the impression of being a prosperous and rising young entrepreneur. He was a member of four London clubs, was accepted in the most exalted company and made sure everyone was aware of it.

He was fortunate to be climbing to the top of the social and financial tree at a time when old Victorian demarcation lines were becoming blurred. Edwardian society was hardly egalitarian, but certain barriers were beginning to break down. Shackleton was not a mere vulgar commercial animal. His business acumen, allied to his supreme self-confidence and considerable social skills, had been his passport out of the bourgeoisie and into more elevated social circles. His position as Dublin Herald also helped his entrée into these circles.

By 1907, he had become part of a sort of transient Anglo-Irish set, some with only the flimsiest of Irish connections, who still showed up in Dublin for occasions like the Castle season or the Royal Dublin Society's Horse Show in August. However, not all his time in England was spent in London. He had passed many weekends in Penshurst in Kent at the home of Lord Ronald Sutherland Gower and Frank Hird.

Sixty-two year old Gower was the best known of Shackleton's new-found friends. The youngest son of the Duke of Sutherland, he had been educated at Eton and Cambridge and was a talented miniaturist as well as an art historian. He had never married but he had taken the unusual step, in 1898, of adopting a grown man as his son. That man was Frank Hird, who had been the foreign correspondent with the *Morning Post* in Rome when Gower met him in 1893. Lord Ronald suffered, periodically, from epilepsy and both he and Hird spent a considerable amount of time in their house, Hammerfield, in Penshurst. Shackleton was a frequent guest, but he was by no means the only one. Another regular visitor was Gower's nephew, the Duke of Argyll. (He and Shackleton spent at least one weekend at Hammerfield together.) Of greater significance, from the point of view of this story, however, is the fact that Argyll was married to Her Royal Highness Princess Louise Caroline Alberta, fourth daughter of Queen Victoria – he was the King's brother-in-law.

On Thursday 4th July, Shackleton had found time to lunch at Lady Ormonde's house in Upper Brook Street. He enjoyed these occasions. Never one to stand around and watch, he liked to join the privileged classes in the enjoyment of their privileges. Probably on account of Shackleton's presence, Sir Arthur Vicars became one of the topics of conversation that day. Someone commented that he was an excessively fussy individual. Shackleton observed that, 'He has a great deal of responsibility and he is very proud of his office.' The subject of the Crown Jewels then arose and Shackleton spoke again. 'Oh,' he ventured, 'I should never be surprised to hear that they were stolen some day. I have never considered them safe.'

The remark may have been tossed off to inject a little controversy into some tepid dining-room chatter. It may, on the other hand, have been an extremely disingenuous comment. It was certainly dropped at an unfortunate juncture in an inappropriate setting. Shackleton chose to publicise his unease with the security arrangements at the Office of Arms a mere two days before the theft of the jewels was discovered, to a roomful of people who would have occasion to dine out on the comment themselves during future social engagements.

His remark had not come back to haunt him when he left for Hammerfield that weekend, but he must have remembered it when his lordship handed him a morning paper on the train back to London on Monday 8th July. Gower pointed to the story of the theft of the jewels. When they reached London, Shackleton immediately sent a telegram to Vicars asking was the newspaper report true. The reply was: 'Yes… and if you have a copy of the Statutes of the Order take them to Scotland Yard to have blocks made of those plates.'

Scotland Yard had no particular interest in the arcane Statutes of the Order of St Patrick. They wanted to copy the drawings of the jewels that the volume contained. As Shackleton had a copy of the Statutes in his London home, he did as he was asked. After passing on the document, Shackleton began to prepare for his departure to Dublin. If he had been hoping that his lunchtime faux pas of the previous Thursday would be forgotten, he was out of luck. One of the first people to greet him when he stepped on board the Dublin mail packet was Lady Ormonde herself. When she spotted Shackleton, she made a beeline for him. 'Oh, Mr Shackleton,' she gushed. 'How extraordinary. Poor Sir Arthur Vicars, I am sorry for him. Isn't it an odd thing… that remark of yours, at lunch the other day?'

Shackleton had no cause for optimism that Lady Ormonde would be discreet about his inopportune observation.

The third man making his way to Dublin was, in a sense, returning home. Inspector John Kane, from Listowel, County Kerry, had been assigned by Scotland Yard to help the Dublin Metropolitan Police in the investigation. He had been the officer to whom Shackleton had delivered the Statutes. It was to be the first of many meetings between the two men.

Kane had joined the London Metropolitan force in 1874 (he retired in 1911) and was considered 'dogged' in his approach to his work. However, he was also, according to some colleagues, 'temperamental' and 'was never happy unless he had a grievance'. The conduct of the Crown Jewels investigation gave him ample opportunity to indulge his testier inclinations. Before his death in 1915, he was to remark to a friend, 'I might have solved it if there hadn't been so many amateur detectives in Dublin while I was there, and if there hadn't been so many clues.'

Frank Shackleton's discomfiture upon his arrival in Kingstown was different in nature to that of Bennett Goldney the previous day. He was less concerned with seasickness than with what certain parties might make of the story with which Lady Ormonde would undoubtedly regale them before she left for her home in Kilkenny.

At around this time, Shackleton fixed on the idea that he would anticipate the gossip by spreading it himself. He hoped to be able to disarm Vicars and Goldney by telling them the story as an amusing anecdote. On that Tuesday morning, 9th July, the three men had breakfast together and, sometime before breakfast, Shackleton broached the subject of the comments he had made in London. He dressed up the episode by focusing on the coincidence of meeting Lady Ormonde on the boat after having made his unguarded remarks. The camouflage was flimsy. Vicars ignored the packaging and attacked the contents. 'Well if you thought they were so unsafe why didn't you ever speak of it to me?' he demanded of Shackleton.

Goldney interjected. 'Why did you think they were unsafe?' And, more pointedly, 'Why did you say such an extraordinary thing at such a peculiar time?'

Shackleton was flustered. He should have been more prepared for this kind of inquisition. 'Because the office was left at night and because it was so lonely,' he observed lamely. To Goldney's second question he made no answer.

The discussion didn't improve Vicars' temper very much. The previous day, Monday 8th July, had not been a good one for him. Kerr had been one of the first visitors to the Bedford Tower that morning and had suggested to Sir Arthur that 'it is a wonder you didn't report the finding of the door of the strong-room open on Saturday morning even after the jewels had been missed'. Vicars took refuge once again in his excuse for having handed Stivey the key of the safe. He said he was 'thronged owing to the preparing for the King's visit'.

Later the same day, the first of two experts arrived. He was Mr F J O'Hare of Milner's Safe Company Ltd and he had come to examine the lock of the strong-room door. For three-and-a-half hours he worked, detaching the lock from the door, dismantling and examining it and then reassembling the whole thing. His opinion was of vital importance to the police. Had the lock been picked or had it been opened with a key? O'Hare told them it could not possibly have been picked. The lock, an expensive one, had a shiny scratch-free surface. Any attempt to pick the lock would have left crude scratches. The lock had to have been opened with a key.

However, it had not, claimed O'Hare, been opened by a key made from a wax impression. Such a key would have opened the door, but would have left some trace. The pressure of the less than perfect copy would have been visible on the levers. The lock had been opened either by its own key or by a copy made from the original.

On Tuesday 9th July, the lock of the safe was examined in the same way by one Cornelius Gallagher. He spent two-and-a-half hours examining the Ratner lock as meticulously as O'Hare had checked the Milner on the strong-room door. He, too, pointed to an unblemished surface and insisted that this ruled out a wax impression. Whoever had opened the lock had done so with its own key or an exact facsimile. To make such a replica, a skilled locksmith would have needed to spend an entire day working on it, and he would have needed the original key with him during that time.

Kerr called back to the Office of Arms at five o'clock on Monday 8th. He had been sent, by Superintendent Lowe, along with his colleague, Cummins, to make a thorough search of the Bedford Tower. They were, Lowe had insisted, to be accompanied by Vicars when making the search. Vicars told the two policemen that the time was inconvenient. He had to leave for the Viceregal Lodge there and then to meet with Lord Aberdeen. Kerr and Cummins arranged that they would make the search at ten thirty the following morning, Tuesday 9th July.

We don't know what happened at the meeting between Vicars and Aberdeen. There may have been some recriminations on the part of Aberdeen, but it is unlikely. He was a benign and an accommodating soul and not the type to rant and upbraid. But, whatever happened (and it is worth speculating on later), Vicars emerged from the conference more buoyant than he had been for some time.

When Vicars returned from the Viceregal Lodge, Kerr was still in the Office of Arms. Not even this was sufficient to dampen Sir Arthur's spirits. 'I would not be a bit surprised,' Vicars told Kerr, 'that they would be returned to my house by parcel post tomorrow morning. His Excellency this evening said the same thing.'

It was a strange remark to make. Upon what grounds did Vicars and Aberdeen base their optimism? They could hardly have expected conscience to make fools of the thieves. Whoever had taken the jewels had put a lot of preparation, planning and careful thought into the operation. It is a fact, unfortunate no doubt but nonetheless true, that thieves tend to be driven by the profit motive. They rarely return their spoils with a note of apology.

Whatever prompted Vicars and Aberdeen to take such a positive approach, the former was sufficiently convinced to remain on in his house until after midday on Tuesday 9th July, the morning of the altercation with the recently returned Shackleton. The argument and the subsequent wait did little to sweeten Vicars' temper. If he expected the postman to knock on the door and cheerily ask him to sign for the Crown Jewels, he was to be disappointed. He remained in Clonskeagh, until long after the post would have come and gone, to no avail.

Vicars reached the Office of Arms at twelve thirty, Shackleton and Goldney were already there. Detective Kerr had been waiting for two hours. Short of pulling up the floorboards, the tower was searched as thoroughly as possible. Vicars took the books in the library from their presses and each volume was examined, as were the presses themselves. Down in the basement, every lump of coal was moved individually and every block of wood was shifted, but nothing of consequence was found.

Meanwhile, the gentlemen of the press had not been idle. Some reports of the theft had appeared on Monday 8th. Many of these were skimpy but, by Tuesday, most papers had fleshed out the story. They recounted the details in that prosaic style that tended to bury the lead somewhere in the fifth paragraph amidst descriptions of the tribulations encountered by 'your correspondent' in eliciting the information. The newspapermen had, in fact, had considerable difficulty in eliciting anything worthwhile from anybody. Castle officials were ducking out of sight to avoid reporters.

As hard news was not available, different papers handled the situation in their different ways. *The Times* gave details of the security arrangements in the Castle: 'The headquarters of the Dublin Metropolitan Police, the headquarters of the Dublin detective force, the headquarters of the Royal Irish Constabulary and the head office of the Dublin military garrison are all within a radius of fifty yards of the Office of Arms. In a word, there is no spot in Dublin, or possibly in the United Kingdom, which is at all hours of the twenty four, more constantly and systematically occupied by soldiers and policemen.'

The Irish Times simply reprinted the statement issued by Castle officials. It contained all sorts of exciting information, such as a detailed description of the jewels, which left behind a vague impression of a lot of harps, loops and shamrocks. As an Irish paper, *The Irish Times* was of the view that the crime was down to perfidious English thieves. 'It is generally believed that the burglary was planned in London,' it hypothesised baselessly. It also took its customary lumps out of the Liberal Party-led Castle authorities and hit an all time low for adverbs when it cried: 'How any person could, unobserved, burglariously enter the Office of Arms, which is exactly opposite the State entrance to the Viceregal apartments, passes all ordinary comprehension.'

Of course, by lying low, the Castle authorities made an important error. As any latter-day public relations expert could tell them, they simply fuelled speculation. In other words, they gave the reporters, correspondents, special correspondents and hacks carte blanche to garnish a minimum of facts with a maximum of imagination and invention. Accusations were levelled at the Irish government and the police that they had something to hide and were carrying on a cover up. At this point, neither the DMP nor the Irish executive had anything in particular they needed to conceal. They would have been better advised to have given journalists something they could use.

On 9th July, Superintendent Lowe sent a report on the robbery to the office of Augustine Birrell, the Chief Secretary. From it, we can discern the direction the investigation was taking. The detectives had, apparently, drawn the obvious conclusions from what they had seen and heard over the previous three days. Lowe commented in the report:

> *Sir Arthur Vicars seems very positive about having locked this safe on the last occasion, previous to the larceny, on which he had been to it, and appears disposed to think that some expert thief had succeeded in opening it by a false key. This theory would, however, hardly be borne out by the circumstances… it appears improbable that any outside person who knew nothing of the building could gain access without leaving marks behind indicating how the entrance had been effected. The facts as at present known would appear to indicate that the larceny was committed by some person familiar with the place who had ordinary means of access, and was aware that the jewels were kept there. If this be the*

correct theory, the safe must have been either left open, or access was had by some surreptitious means to Sir Arthur Vicars' keys.

The Dublin police were pointing the finger, not at London safe-crackers but at someone connected with the Office of Arms.

The DMP also asked for a reward of £1,000 to be offered for 'such information as will lead to the recovery of the jewels'. The usually tightfisted Treasury Department approved the expenditure (which has yet to be claimed). The amount offered didn't represent a very generous percentage of the value of the stolen gems. The official estimate of their worth was £31,050. The Star was said to be worth £14,000, the Badge £16,000 and the five collars totalled £1,050. In addition, Vicars put a value of £1,500 on his mother's jewels. The police valuation is reckoned by many to have been an underestimate. Some, at the time, put the value of the jewels at nearer £50,000. Given gem inflation through the last century, they would be worth in excess of €1,000,000 today.

On 10th July, King Edward VII arrived with his impressive entourage in train. He was accompanied by his Secretary Lord Knollys, his Lord Chamberlain Lord Althorp, his Minister-in-Waiting, his Lord-in-Waiting, his Groom-in-Waiting and two Equerries-in-Waiting. Queen Alexandra's complement was, by those standards, comparatively modest. She did, however, have with her a Lady-of-the-Bedchamber and a Woman-of-the-Bedchamber.

King Edward had barely stepped onto dry land when the subject Aberdeen most wanted to avoid was broached. Aberdeen was wearing what were called the 'undress insignia'. Put simply, these were third-rate baubles worn during daylight hours or on less formal occasions. When the King came ashore, he began scrutinising the Badge of the Order of St Patrick being worn by his representative in Ireland. Aberdeen began to worry that the Badge was affixed upside down or something equally non-viceregal.

He asked, 'Is it not right, Sir?'

'Oh, yes,' replied the King, 'but I was thinking of those jewels.' Having made his point within half a minute of landing, the King dropped the subject.

At about the time the King was attending Leopardstown Races on the day of his arrival, the police were slogging around Dublin asking locksmiths whether anybody had asked them to fashion keys that would have fitted either the safe or the strong-room of the Office of Arms. They drew a blank.

On 11th July, when *The Irish Times* suggested that the King's visit to Leopardstown Races had made 'more harmonious the intimate relations that exist and must always exist between the integral parts of the central system of Empire', members of the Dublin Metropolitan Police were circularising pawnbrokers in London with handbills depicting the jewels and a detective was doing likewise in Amsterdam. Despite their earnest efforts, the investigation was at a standstill. However, there were high hopes that the arrival of Inspector Kane of Scotland Yard would get things moving again.

The first person to whom Kane spoke was Dublin Castle's

chief investigating officer Superintendent Lowe, who briefed him comprehensively. Next, he questioned Sir Arthur Vicars. He asked Vicars to explain to him about the ribbon that had been left behind in the red morocco case. Vicars intimated that it would have required both familiarity with the Badge and a certain amount of time to manipulate the ribbon. Kane had, apparently, already decided that this was the case because, pointing to Lowe he told Vicars, 'If my opinion is worth anything… this gentleman must remain to look for the thief in this building, because what has been described to me would be utterly impossible, to my mind, on the part of an ordinary outside thief.'

The presence of the ribbon and the fact that the paper in which the collars were wrapped had been neatly folded and returned to the boxes were the features of the case that had struck Kane most forcibly. 'Experience teaches,' he would later observe, 'that when a thief secures his booty in another man's house, the first thing uppermost in his mind is to secure his retreat. What does he care whether cases are restored? He wants to get away.' Kane's message was clear. The thief, quite plainly was not 'in another man's house' but on familiar ground. Face to face with Kane and Lowe, Vicars was shaken by what the Scotland Yard man was saying. He stonewalled. 'I have implicit confidence in every member of my staff,' he insisted.

Kane then asked Vicars to offer his own theory. Flying in the face of the known facts (for which he had something of a talent), Vicars suggested that someone had got a wax impression of his keys and had stolen the jewels. Kane reminded him of the opinions of the two locksmiths. He then singled out the strong-room door incident as proof of his theory. It was reasonable to assume, the inspector surmised, that whoever had gone to the trouble of opening the strong-room door would have gone inside. Vicars conceded that this was a reasonable assumption.

'If an outside thief did that,' Kane continued, 'will you please suggest why he did not secure some of the property there, such as the gold crown and the collection of valuable articles up on the shelf of an ordinary press, with ordinary glass in it, and I understand that even the key of the press was kept in the drawer of the table in the middle of the room.'

Kane had done his homework well. Vicars fumbled for an answer. 'He was disturbed,' he ventured. 'He must have been disturbed.'

'By whom, or by what?' asked the detective. 'You will recollect the leisurely way in which he operated at the safe. There was no hurry there. He was in the seclusion of a small strong-room at the back of a large and unoccupied house. What disturbed him? If disturbed, who chased him? Where did he go? How did he disappear? Has anybody picked up any stolen property that he dropped in his flight?'

'No, no,' said Vicars. 'I cannot account for that at all.'

'To my mind,' continued Kane, 'the man who did that has a knowledge of this building.' Vicars, who had been personally responsible for the appointment of virtually everyone connected with the Office of Arms, was beaten back to his last line of defence. 'I reiterate,' he protested. 'I have implicit confidence in every member of my staff!' Then the three men went down to view the scene of the crime.

For the first time, Kane was shown the ribbon on which he had based much of his hypothesis. Vicars explained to him exactly how long it would have taken to manipulate it. Kane had felt, on reading the DMP reports, that the suggestion of five minutes for this operation might have been somewhat exaggerated. He was surprised to find that it was not. It served to reinforce his theory. For his part, in spite of having indicated earlier that whoever had removed the ribbon and stolen the Badge must have been familiar with it, Vicars clung tenaciously to the defence of his staff.

On Friday 12th July, Vicars approached Superintendent Lowe with an unusual request. Lowe had appropriated one of Vicars' safe keys for himself shortly after the discovery of the robbery. He had taken the key that Vicars habitually carried around and asked him to make do with the one he had hidden in his desk. Now, for some reason that he didn't explain, Vicars wanted to swop keys.

Lowe was curious and asked Vicars why he needed that particular key. Vicars, it transpired, had had a visit from a lady connected with the Italian section of the Dublin International Exhibition. The lady had told him that she could help him trace the lost jewels. Her daughter was psychic, she claimed, and was having visions that were leading her to the jewels. If she could touch something associated with the gems, she might be able to locate them. Vicars was prepared to try anything.

On Sunday 14th July, a group of hopeful spiritualists assembled in St James' Terrace. The safe key that Vicars had retrieved from Lowe was placed in the middle of a table and the principals gathered round to wait for the medium to get the message. This particular key had been chosen for its greater resonance and the result was a resounding success. The young lady conjured up a vision. The Crown Jewels, she informed Vicars, were concealed near a tombstone not far from the entrance to an old disused churchyard near Clonsilla in northwest County Dublin.

The following day, Vicars told the police what had happened. They may have been sceptical but they were also desperate. Not only did they give the whole charade their blessing, but they offered the services of a policeman to help with the search. The officer accompanied Vicars and Pierce Gun Mahony on the treasure hunt. They combed the Clonsilla graveyard without result. They even looked for signs of freshly dug earth. Discouraged, but not totally disillusioned, they headed for another old churchyard near Mulhuddart, a short distance away. They drew a blank there as well.

The youthful clairvoyant did not accompany the three men on their search. She showed remarkable vision in that respect at least.

Shortly after his return from the Clonsilla cemetery hunt, a journalist succeeded in buttonholing Vicars and getting him to answer some questions. His report of the conversation appeared in the Dublin *Daily Express* and makes interesting reading. Vicars, for example, insisted that 'there is only one key to the safe and here it is… it has never left my possession, and if the theory is entertained that a wax impression of it has been obtained extraordinary ingenuity must have been displayed by whoever secured it'. He neglected to mention the existence of the second key.

He also told the reporter that 'only two persons had a key to the strong-room and he was one of them'. Another untruth; as we know, there were four keys and, at the time of the robbery, three people had one in their possession. He was asked if he thought the robbery had been carried out by expert thieves and replied, 'I can't, of course, express any opinion as to what the police think. It goes without saying that somebody with an intimate knowledge of the premises must have taken the jewels, but that does not necessarily indicate that it must have been someone resident in Dublin.' The first part of the statement represented a significant concession both to reality and expert opinion. The second part was a defensive response to an unasked question.

More amusingly, Vicars went on to reveal that he had had an offer of help from Sir Arthur Conan Doyle, a distant cousin. The creator of Sherlock Holmes had written to Vicars offering his advice. The *Express* commented: 'We are afraid that it would offer him material for a story rather than that he would offer us some material for a discovery. But... it is rash to disparage the real Sherlock Holmes.'

The *Express* also reported, and commented upon, a curious fact. Vicars had taken the opportunity presented by the interview to suggest to the thief that there was little possibility of disposing of his plunder and that the best thing he could do was to return the jewels by parcel post and claim the reward. The *Express* ritually applauded Vicars' appeal but added, presciently, that: 'It is hardly compatible with the theory that the robbery is the work of professional jewel thieves. One can only hope that Sir Arthur has some definite reason for putting forward his suggestion for, if the thieves were really professional cracksmen, it would be useless to make such an appeal. To them the claiming of the reward would be merely putting their heads into the lion's den.'

Did Vicars, in spite of his avowed opinion, really believe that the crime might have been committed by an amateur? Perhaps even by someone well known to him who might be keeping the jewels with a view to seeking ransom? Did he have a 'definite reason' for making the suggestion as the *Express* intimated? Could he have been offering a way out for a member of his staff?

The final Scotland Yard interview of the Crown Jewels investigation took place in England, at the home of the antiquarian J C Hodgson, who simply confirmed what he had already told the police by telegram – that he had seen the jewels on 11th June. By then, Kane had returned to London and, to outside appearances, the police were baffled and the trail was getting cold. Appearances, however, were deceptive. The police had discovered quite a lot. In fact, they had found out more than they had bargained for.

The old adage about turning over a stone and waiting to see what crawls out from underneath has great relevance in this case. The investigation now entered its murky phase. Just as the press, with no facts at its disposal, invented and speculated, so it was with Dublin Castle society when the subject of the jewels was discussed. Malevolent rumours began to circulate in the upper echelons, some inspired and untrue, others uninspiring and true. None of those involved in the case emerged with the odour of blossoms clinging to them.

Within a few days of championing the innocence of his staff in his discussion with Inspector Kane, Vicars had begun to change his mind. Whispers had reached him about the man he had appointed Dublin Herald, Francis Shackelton. In the light of the jewel theft, Vicars was warned by friends that Shackelton was a 'shady character' and not to be trusted. The vague feeling that his own position was in some jeopardy inclined Vicars towards seeking out a more credible scapegoat for the crime than the Board of Works. The lack of progress in the investigation depressed him. If the guilty party remained undetected, pressure might be applied from certain quarters for heads to roll. In that event, his must certainly be one of the first to go.

Vicars began to wonder aloud about Shackleton's lunchtime remarks in London on the security of the jewels. He started to question the timing of the comments. Were they as innocent as Shackleton had made them out to be?

By 2nd August 1907, Vicars told Kane, who was on a return visit to Dublin, that he now agreed with him completely. He was prepared to accept that the crime had been committed by someone well acquainted with the Office of Arms. However, he did not suggest any candidates to the detective at that juncture. Shortly after making the observation, Vicars himself left for England. He had been under severe strain for over three weeks and his friend Bennett Goldney had invited him to Canterbury.

Frank Shackleton was in better health than Vicars, but then he was a far more phlegmatic individual to begin with. During August, he was relaxing in Harrogate when his attention was drawn to a newspaper story. The paper reported that the jewels had been found and restored. Annoyed at having had to read about this development at the breakfast table, Shackleton wrote to Vicars and Pierce Gun Mahony demanding to know why he had not been informed. Later, he met Bennett Goldney at one of his London clubs and made the same point to him.

As it happened, the newspaper report was complete nonsense, the jewels had not been recovered. However, Shackleton's letter reinforced Vicars' growing prejudices. He and Goldney had discussed Shackleton many times during his sojourn in Canterbury and they had succeeded in convincing one another that Shackleton had been involved in the crime. Twisting what Shackleton had said beyond recognition, Goldney now visited Inspector Kane in Scotland Yard and told him that Shackleton knew of the whereabouts of the jewels.

At the same time, Vicars wrote Shackleton a letter. It dealt mainly with financial arrangements between them. One paragraph stands out: '…now that you evidently know the whereabouts of the jewels from what you have said to both Frank [Bennett Goldney] and me, I hope that you have told Mr Kane everything calculated to facilitate matters.' In other words, now that Shackleton had admitted to having stolen the jewels, Vicars and Goldney fondly wished that he'd be a good boy and turn himself in.

The tone of that particular letter might have led Shackleton to assume that Sir Arthur was joking, although the self-important Vicars was not noted for his sense of humour, but Shackleton did not realise until some days later that Goldney and Vicars were convinced that he had stolen the jewels. By which time, the two men had done considerable damage.

That Vicars had not been joking was brought home forcefully to Shackleton because of another bizarre twist to the plot. On 28th August, Lord Aberdeen, the Lord Lieutenant himself, had received an anonymous telegram from Great Malvern in London saying: 'Jewels are in box, 9 Hadley St, Dublin.' Unfortunately for all concerned, Dublin did not have a Hadley Street. So it was assumed that the telegram had been mischievously intended to mislead the police.

Around the time the telegram was sent, Shackleton was in

Southsea. He returned to London towards the beginning of the following week (2nd September) and visited one of his clubs. He was surprised when Inspector Kane was ushered into his presence. Kane asked Shackleton to accompany him to Scotland Yard where he had something he wanted him to see. When the two men arrived in Kane's office, the policeman produced the original of the Hadley Street telegram. It was folded over on itself so that only the word 'Dublin' was visible. 'Whose writing is that?' asked the detective.

Shackleton studied it for a moment. 'That is mine,' he replied.

Kane opened out the telegram. Shackleton looked at it again. He then changed his mind, he had not written the telegram after all. The word 'Dublin', he insisted, had borne a superficial resemblance to his hand but, when he saw the full telegram, he realised the writing was not his. Kane thanked him for his co-operation and telegraphed Canterbury requesting Sir Arthur Vicars to come to Scotland Yard on a matter of some urgency. Vicars responded immediately and was there within hours. With Shackleton present, he was shown as much of the telegram as Shackleton had seen and was asked who had written the word 'Dublin'. He looked at Shackleton. 'I suppose you did,' he said.

The message was then opened out for him as it had been for Shackleton. Vicars continued to claim that his colleague had written the telegram.

'You don't believe it's mine, do you?' Shackleton asked.

'Yes I do', was the emphatic reply.

'You may think the writing is like mine but you don't think I wrote it, do you?'

'I do think you wrote it,' insisted Vicars, 'and that you have not assisted the police.'

'Now, Mr Shackleton,' Inspector Kane said, 'you will not be astonished at whatever action the police may take.'

Shackleton was shattered. By his own account, he had not dreamed up till then that he was under suspicion of any kind. The next few days were spent waiting for the inevitable summons for further questioning. In addition, Vicars and Bennett Goldney had not been keeping their suspicions to themselves. Word had got out quickly that Shackleton was being investigated. He became an object of rampant gossip and curiosity. He was only to be let off the hook by another clairvoyant.

On 4th September, Aberdeen received a second communication from Great Malvern. This one was signed, by a Mr Bullock Webster, and explained that he had sent the anonymous telegram the week before. He had done so because his wife had had a vision relating to the jewels in which she had seen the words '9 Hadley St, Dublin'. He had sent the telegram to be helpful, but had not signed it because he did not wish to draw attention to himself.

In fact, he could not have called more attention to himself if he'd tried. He was questioned closely, as was his wife. Finally, the police accepted his story, that he was an honest citizen trying to be of service. Shackleton could breathe a long sigh of relief. But he would have been far less easy in his mind had he known of certain facts about himself that had been turned up by the investigation into the loss of the regalia.

5

'Star Chamber'

> *You sit with your friends, hugging your knees and smoking your pipe, and you talk about – what? Sport, politics! Woman might not exist; she is bad form. An evening in London now and then, I daresay… then back to this male life among a thousand other young men, as though nothing had happened. Yes, you are a strange race, a secret race, ashamed of being natural.*
>
> *The Edwardians* Vita Sackville-West

KING EDWARD VII thought about the jewels quite a lot. On his brief visit to Ireland, he had made his displeasure at their disappearance manifestly clear to Aberdeen almost as the words of welcome had died on the Lord Lieutenant's lips. They were, after all, Crown Jewels, and had been a gift from his granduncle William IV to the Knights of St Patrick – the King felt their loss and took a keen interest in the investigation into their disappearance.

Not that there was much happening to help maintain his interest. Lord Aberdeen kept the King's Secretary, Lord Knollys, supplied with occasional non-committal progress reports. Suspecting he was being fobbed off, the King became increasingly restless. Knollys wrote to Aberdeen on 26th August 1907, saying that the King was of the opinion: '...that there is a mystery and an apparent lukewarmness about the Enquiry and in fact the whole proceedings which he does not understand. He says that at the end of nearly two months, surely if there is ever to be a clue it must have been discovered by this time.'

Knollys also started a process, which very quickly acquired momentum, when he wrote: 'His Majesty also says somebody must have been careless in their care of these Crown Jewels, and if so he would be glad to know whom, and whether, whoever it may be, anything in the way of punishment or reprimand has been given to him.'

Four days later, Aberdeen was able to report some progress. He had spoken to Police Commissioner Sir John Ross and his deputy, M V Harrel, and had been told by them that the police were now concentrating their attention on 'those who had means of access to the jewels; and not only to those persons but to others who, from time to time, have associated with them'. Ross and Harrel had asked Aberdeen to be patient. 'The tracing, with the necessary discretion, of the habits, proceedings and associates of people who occupy some sort of social position is of course a very delicate business, and it is necessary to accumulate a great deal before there can be any justification for actual proceedings.'

Aberdeen then informed Knollys that 'suspicions have been directed towards one of the junior members of the herald's staff'.

It is apparent from subsequent correspondence that the junior member in question was Shackleton. Inspector Kane was clearly dubious about Shackleton, but the police were unwilling to focus too overtly on him because of a commendable sensitivity about the consequences for the Dublin Herald of any of their suspicions getting into the public domain. 'The Commissioner [Ross] begged,' Aberdeen wrote, 'that he might not as yet be asked to mention the name, for fear that if the suspicions are not verified, a stigma, which might be undeserved, should rest upon the man.' But while Ross was being discreet, Vicars and Goldney were not.

Ross based the information he gave Aberdeen on the preliminary findings of Inspector Kane. Before his initial departure from Dublin, Kane had filed a report on the outcome of his investigation. He had discussed its contents verbally with the ranking officials of the DMP and submitted a written account of his findings to his own superiors in Scotland Yard. The report was dated 16th July 1907 and, as with so much else connected with this case, it is cloaked in mystery. There would have been at least two copies of this crucial report, one for Dublin Castle and one for Scotland Yard. Neither exists today.

It looks very much as if both copies of the report were meticulously removed from Home Office and Chief Secretary for Ireland files. But we are still left with some tantalising clues as to its contents. Towards the end of 1912, five years later, a series of parliamentary questions from the Irish nationalist (later Sinn Féin) MP Laurence Ginnell was directed at the Chief Secretary, Augustine Birrell, designed to elicit from him the contents of the report. However, Birrell was not forthcoming; his civil-service briefs still exist and, in conjunction with a slip up from Birrell himself, tell us something about this enigmatic report.

The documentation, related to a Ginnell parliamentary question of 12th December 1912, confirms that the DMP received Kane's written report in January 1908. A 1912 memo in the relevant file, which Birrell would have read in preparation for the question, claims that: 'Kane mentioned no names of persons concerned in the stealing or receiving of the Crown Jewels. He arrived, as a result of his investigations, at the same conclusion as the DMP, that the theft was the work of some person or persons having an intimate knowledge of the Office of Arms but though the police have followed up every clue neither then nor since have they been able to obtain a particle of evidence implicating any individual in the transaction.'

But the terse memo conceals as much as it reveals because Kane *had* mentioned some names, albeit in a different context to the remit of his original investigation. How do we know? Because Ginnell wouldn't leave the subject of the Crown Jewels alone. He came back to the issue the following month. Birrell slipped up when he was faced, during Question Time on 16th January 1913, with Ginnell's parliamentary interrogation. Birrell had a notoriously low boredom threshold and, by 1913, he had other things on his mind. The whole subject of the Crown Jewels was, no doubt, becoming tedious. As a result of his ennui, he effectively admitted that Kane had included some names in his report.

Ginnell asked the Chief Secretary why no criminal proceedings had been instituted against any of the people implicated in the report of Detective Inspector Kane 'on his special business in Ireland in 1907'.

The exchange continued as follows.

MR BIRRELL: 'As I have already stated no criminal proceedings were instituted because there was no evidence to justify such proceedings.'

MR GINNELL: 'That is not the answer to the question on the paper. Will the Right Honourable gentleman answer the question on the paper?'

MR BIRRELL: 'I think I have.'

MR GINNELL: 'Why were no criminal proceedings taken against the persons implicated in this inspector's report?'

MR BIRRELL: 'The Honourable Member may choose to say that they were implicated; all I can say is there was no evidence to justify the Executive taking any proceedings *against any of the persons named* [my italics].'

So why, in his report on the theft, did Kane identify people who were not necessarily implicated in the theft? His brief was specific. He was to look into the disappearance of the jewels and make known his findings to the Dublin authorities. What other reasons had he for naming people in the report who were not involved in the theft? As we shall see, there were significant reasons why he had done so.

At the beginning of the 20th century, society did not consider homosexuality to be an 'inclination' or an 'orientation', it was simply a 'perversion'. Because of this prevailing attitude, there was an understandable reserve on the part of Edwardians to discuss the subject. It was something people preferred to think did not happen and that instinct was encouraged by the establishment when some of its own were involved in potential homosexual scandals. The essential thing was to keep all salacious information within a tight circle and out of the public domain. The hoi polloi were not to be treated to bad examples from their betters.

Which brings us back to those two copies of Inspector Kane's mysterious report.

What had happened was this. In looking into the theft of the Crown Jewels in Dublin, Inspector Kane found himself involved in a parallel investigation into the activities of highly placed homosexuals in the city. As some of those implicated in this scandal were the same people who were under scrutiny in connection with the disappearance of the jewels, Kane linked the two investigations. There is also some evidence (of an anecdotal nature only) that a similar scandal was being kept under wraps in London and that there was at least one individual common to both groups. Kane had no solid proof that any of the names mentioned in connection with homosexuality had anything to do with the theft of the jewels but, as homosexual activity was a crime in 1907, they were technically guilty of indictable offences.

If Kane did not identify any suspects in his missing report, why is it missing? Perhaps it was because he had introduced evidence of the existence of the group of homosexuals associated with the Office of Arms and added it as a rider to his report. This supposition is the thrust of Ginnell's question of January 1913. His supplementary question was far more apposite. When he asked, 'Why were no criminal proceedings taken against the persons implicated in the inspector's report?', he was not referring to those responsible for the theft of the jewels but to those accused of the indictable 'crime' of engaging in homosexual activities.

Documented allusions to homosexual activity at the Office of Arms are oblique and names are seldom used. The written communications between the likes of Aberdeen and Knollys were often followed up with more detailed verbal briefings that elaborated on the coded language used in the written reports. But, from the clear references that are made, it is apparent that Shackleton's homosexuality soon became known to Kane, as did his relationship with well-connected homosexuals in London. It was partly for this reason that he also became the chief suspect in the robbery investigation. The reasoning was that, even if he had not actually stolen the jewels himself (he was out of the country when they were taken), he might, under threat of exposure as a homosexual, have been blackmailed into supplying the thieves with the sort of help and information that had ensured the success of their operation.

King Edward had already expressed his annoyance at the delay in recovering the jewels about two months after their disappearance. When another month passed without any positive result, he not only became more exasperated, he became highly suspicious. He concluded that something other than a lack of evidence was stalling the investigation.

Lord Knollys wrote to Aberdeen on 17th September 1907: 'The King knows that you personally, are anxious that the mystery of this audacious robbery should be cleared up, and the blame fastened on the proper shoulders; but it does not appear to His Majesty that the feeling is universal, and the inquiry... seems to be dawdling on in a somewhat leisurely fashion.'

Aberdeen was caught in the middle. The position of Lord Lieutenant was largely a ceremonial and insubstantial one without much authority or influence. He would be kept informed by the DMP of what was going on, but he could also be fobbed off very easily. He had no option but to acquiesce when Harrel or Ross told him that progress was being made but that, for fear of retarding the enquiries, they couldn't be too forthcoming on the trend of the investigation.

Aberdeen then had to dress this up and sell it to the King – who obviously wasn't buying. As a result, Aberdeen felt under considerable stress and decided to exert some pressure of his own. It yielded results. Four days later, on 21st September, he presented the King with something a little more substantial than 'please be patient'. He wrote requesting an audience, explaining that he had obtained a secret police report (probably from Harrel, based loosely on Kane's information) and that 'several names are mentioned as being under suspicion in connection with the affair (including the names of two men who are, or have been, officers in the army or, rather, the militia)'.

The following day, Knollys replied, granting Aberdeen's request for a conference with the King and added: '…the King is not surprised to hear of the very *disagreeable disclosures* [my italics] which appear to be forthcoming as he was sure there were features in the case which caused it to hang fire under investigation in the unaccountable way it has done.' Aberdeen's letter says nothing whatsoever about any 'disagreeable disclosures' or any reason for the enquiry to have been stalled. It is reasonable to assume that Aberdeen's letter was accompanied by an enclosure of some kind that has not made its way into the correspondence file in the Royal Archive in Windsor Castle. This enclosure cannot have been very specific but it would have told the King all Aberdeen knew. Something had happened to hamper the investigation. A few days later, Aberdeen received more detailed and graphic information about exactly what that impediment was.

On 28th September, Aberdeen had a long conversation with Harrel and what he heard from the Assistant Commissioner shocked him. He saw immediately that here was a scandal potentially serious enough to shake the government, and perhaps even lead to a host of high-level resignations. Harrel told Aberdeen that, after office hours, it was the habit of Vicars to offer hospitality in the Bedford Tower to his acquaintances. There he would unwind, along with some of the junior heralds and many of the leading civil servants working in the Castle. Harrel stopped short of depicting Babylonian orgies, but gave Aberdeen to understand that, among the guests at Vicars' soirees, were some of Dublin's leading homosexuals. Furthermore, Aberdeen's own son, Lord Haddo, was a frequent guest at these informal functions.

Aberdeen was alarmed at Harrel's revelations and at the mileage that could be extracted from this information by the

Irish Parliamentary Party and other nationalist elements. By the time they had finished shouting 'buggery' from the opposition benches, everybody who had ever set foot in the Office of Arms during the hours of darkness would have been dubbed a sodomist.

He wrote an anxious letter to Knollys. He didn't trust himself to commit too much to paper, but the little he did write is revealing. He wanted the King to hear all the details from Harrel himself. He told Knollys of his long interview with Harrel 'which has made evident the extraordinary manner in which this case is complicated by what has transpired during the primary investigations'.

The letter became almost paranoid when it dealt with ways of ensuring that any conference between Harrel and the King was kept under wraps. Aberdeen would entertain Harrel at his Scottish estate for a few days and, during that period, 'if the King were disposed to motor over' (from Balmoral) nobody would see any 'special significance' in the visit.

Aberdeen was extremely vague about why exactly such a meeting was necessary, and why it should take place in such secrecy. Just in case Knollys might feel he was overreacting and refuse his request, Aberdeen wrote that: '…the complications referred to are in connection with the suspicions (which I find are more than suspicions) of scandalous conduct. Of that particular sort about which every now and then some painful reference is made and which has at times been such a source of anxiety in some of our public schools.' Aberdeen was being suitably coy, but he certainly was not referring to the degenerate Edwardian boarding school tradition of the midnight feast.

So how do we identify the unnamed 'scandalous' men associated with the Office of Arms referred to by Aberdeen? We can assume that the sexual inclinations of the lowlier Office of Arms employees – Burtchaell, Horlock and Stivey – would not have complicated or delayed any investigation. Their lack of any significant social or political connection meant that their exposure would not have had any potentially unfortunate repercussions. They would have been dealt with ruthlessly and expeditiously.

At first, the police seem to have assumed that Vicars himself was involved in homosexual activities. He was, after all, the host of the Bedford Tower soirees. Later, they chose to abandon this belief (but not, as we shall see, until extensive use had been made of the suspicion to discredit him).

Could one of the two men have been the Cork Herald, Pierce Gun Mahony, Vicars' nephew? The short answer is, no. On 14th October, in a crucial letter to the King, Aberdeen effectively exonerates Mahony, writing: '...there remains the case of Mr O'Mahony [sic]... regarding whom there is no slander or suspicion of any kind.'

It is quite clear from the thrust of the extensive correspondence between Aberdeen and Knollys that Frank Shackleton was one of the two men. The other could well have been a disreputable military friend of Shackleton's, Captain Richard Howard Gorges, of whom we will hear much more anon. But, by a process of elimination, we must conclude that the second man was Francis Bennett Goldney. He seems to fit the bill admirably. Like Shackleton, he had served in the militia, rising to the rank of captain in the 6th Militia Battalion, the Middlesex Regiment. Whatever his sexual inclinations, there is no documentary evidence that the police had any serious suspicions of his involvement in the theft of the jewels. If they had, they certainly did not subject him to the same thorough scrutiny as they did Shackleton.

The incident of the Great Malvern telegram deepened official suspicion against Shackleton. Even though somebody else had claimed responsibility for sending the telegram, he was still the subject of an intense investigation. In a letter to Knollys, sent over three weeks after the issue appeared to have been cleared up satisfactorily, Aberdeen wrote that: 'Shackleton can hardly be unaware that the incident of the telegram makes him a marked man and of course there remains a good deal to be cleared up even in regard to this particular item of the case.' At that time, the police were still trying to trap the unfortunate Mr Bullock Webster into admitting that Shackleton had sent the telegram and that he had been paid to cover for him. They also discovered that Shackleton, the normally sure-footed businessman, was having financial trouble – his Midas touch had temporarily deserted him. As Aberdeen informed Knollys, Scotland Yard had found out that he had been visiting London pawnshops in an attempt to raise some cash in a hurry.

Naturally, an entirely different complexion could also be put on those visits. It must have occurred to the police that the Crown Jewels would have made good collateral for a loan from a dishonest broker. Shackleton was watched ever more closely. However, if he had been involved in the theft, it might take much time and patient surveillance before he made a mistake and revealed himself. In the meantime, the police had other pressing matters to deal with.

Aberdeen's letter to King Edward of 14th October that absolved Pierce Gun Mahony of all blame contained much more than an exoneration of the Cork Herald. The letter was a call to action. In essence, it asked the King to agree to the dismissal of Vicars on the grounds of negligence and advocated a comprehensive clean sweep of the Office of Arms, clearing it of all those guilty of 'scandalous conduct'. In the case of the sacking of Shackleton, some diplomatic pretext needed to be found lest anybody be alerted to the real reason for his dismissal. However, Aberdeen recognised that 'the case of Mr Goldney is more difficult, owing partly to the fact that he is the present Mayor of Canterbury'.

After the lengthy period of stasis and immobility that had followed the theft of the Crown Jewels, what had prompted this sudden surge, this injection of purpose into a mire of inactivity?

The King had been the first to record the opinion, on 26th August 1907, that, 'Somebody must have been careless in their care of these Crown Jewels', but the Irish government had not been slow to cast around for someone to blame. Events such as these required a sacrificial victim. Vicars was the obvious candidate. Aberdeen's letter of 14th October was the culmination of a process that had begun shortly after the theft was discovered. Vicars' erratic behaviour on and since 6th July had not impressed the police. Neither had it enthralled Sir Anthony MacDonnell, the Under Secretary for Ireland, or Sir J B Dougherty, the Assistant Under Secretary.

However, in the best traditions of civil-service accountability, it was vital that the damage be contained, limited to the expendables only. When the salvo was finally loosed, the shot must not spread over too wide an area. Persuasive, if not unanswerable, cases could be made for negligence on the part of the Board of Works

– the jewels had been placed in and stolen from a safe they supplied – and the Dublin Metropolitan Police – the robbery had taken place in the most closely guarded area in the country. However, all this had to be somehow glossed over. Vicars would walk the plank on his own, guilty of exercising 'lack of vigilance and care' for the Crown Jewels. And his tormentor, prodding him towards the open sea at sword point, was the King, the man to whom he owed his job.

A letter from Knollys to Aberdeen on 17th September had delivered King Edward's judgement in the most unequivocal terms: 'To sum up, the King considers Ulster King of Arms responsible for the custody of the Insignia, and he alone is to blame for this crisis. The King feels so strongly on this point that unless evidence is forthcoming to clear him it is a question as to whether Sir A Vicars should not be suspended from his office.'

Following that unambiguous message and, in the aftermath of the revelations of 'scandalous conduct' towards the beginning of October 1907, Aberdeen, Birrell, MacDonnell, Dougherty, Ross and Harrel met in secret to decide what to do about Vicars. That the meeting ever took place was always emphatically denied. Champions of Vicars were to call this assembly a 'Star Chamber'. This characterisation was appropriate in every respect except one; even in the days of the Tudor monarchy's notorious Star Chamber interrogations, the accused was given some opportunity to refute the charges against him.

This meeting of the elite of the British administration in Ireland and the police chiefs was called to discuss what steps to take to remove Vicars and return the Office of Arms to some semblance of normality. It was a delicate matter. Publicity had to be avoided, at all costs. The Office of Arms was directly answerable to the King, and Edward VII certainly did not want a homosexual controversy erupting into the open in the manner of a similar scandal that had rocked the court of the German Kaiser just a few months previously. The King had to be distanced from the whole affair. The Office of Arms must be cleaned out without giving a clue that there were any motives other than the justifiable removal of an incompetent administration.

For the first time, the theft of the jewels came as a blessing in disguise. Vicars could be asked for his resignation on the grounds of negligence. Whatever the truth of his own sexual inclinations he had, after all, introduced Shackleton and Goldney, now seen as men of dubious moral reputation, into the Office of Arms.

The case of the three junior heralds – two implicated, one innocent – was not quite so straightforward. They could not be sacked on grounds of 'lack of vigilance and care' as Vicars could. They had had no responsibility at all for the security of the insignia. Getting rid of them because of the disappearance of the jewels wouldn't make sense. A better excuse would have to be found. The consensus seems to have been that the administration would opt for a blanket pretext that would apply to all. For public consumption, the heralds were to be asked to quit because the Office of Arms was to be reconstituted. Their departures would facilitate that reorganisation.

So Aberdeen's letter to the King on 14th October sought his approval for a course of action that needed the King's authority. The 'Star Chamber' recommendation was accepted with alacrity. However, the clean out was not to be absolutely comprehensive. The guiltless Mahony was to be given a carefully engineered, last-minute reprieve, probably at the behest of the soft-hearted

Aberdeen. It was suggested that he be asked to resign *pro tem* but it was to be intimated to him that he would be reinstated when the office was reconstituted. It was assumed that everybody, for his own reasons, would go quietly. Of course, there was still the fear that some interested and informed outside observer would smell a rat. Aberdeen explained to the King 'even with the above suggested mode of dealing with the question of clearing the office, there is likely to be a good deal of unpleasant comment and surmise: which however, it may be hoped, will die down soon'. Aberdeen's hopes were not to be fulfilled.

Arising out of the decision taken by the administration officials and the King's acquiescence in the 'Star Chamber' conclusions, Sir Arthur Vicars received the following letter, dated 23rd October 1907. It was signed, in the absence of MacDonnell, who was on leave, by the Assistant Under Secretary for Ireland.

> *Sir,*
>
> *I am directed by the Lord Lieutenant to inform you that His Excellency has received from the King, His Majesty's approval of the reconstitution of the Office of Arms, Dublin Castle. This will involve your being relieved of the office of Ulster which you now hold.*
>
> *I am therefore to request you to make immediate arrangements for relinquishing the duties of your office.*
>
> *J B Dougherty*

For Vicars, it was both the end of the beginning and the beginning of the end.

During the month of September, Vicars' fixation that Shackleton had stolen the Crown Jewels had grown and he had successfully convinced Goldney too. He tried, without apparent success, to persuade Chief Inspector Kane. All he lacked was a cogent theory. Shackleton had left Dublin for England on 11th June and had not returned until the 9th July. Despite this inconvenient fact, Vicars didn't stint himself in his attempts to impress the DMP with plausible hypotheses all pointing in Shackleton's direction.

Vicars advanced the theory to the DMP that Shackleton had made impressions of all the necessary keys, returned to Dublin secretly, stayed in a hotel in Dublin's North Wall (he even supplied the name of the hotel) and had stolen the jewels on 30th June. Vicars' conclusion was woven out of a mixture of fantasy, hearsay and outright special pleading. For a time, it happened to match the police's thinking. They were highly suspicious of Shackleton, though this is no credit to Vicars, it was merely a happy coincidence. The police's suspicions were born out of thorough investigation rather than supposition and prejudice. The DMP and Scotland Yard eventually abandoned their investigation of Shackleton by November of 1907 (mainly through lack of evidence). However, once it became imbedded, Sir Arthur was never shaken in his belief that his erstwhile friend had stolen the jewels.

Dougherty's dismissal letter of 23rd October 1907 seems to have had a peculiar effect on Vicars. He had been under considerable strain and his behaviour to date had been erratic and at times malicious (as his coachman, Phillips, and Shackleton could attest). As time went on and the Crown Jewels remained missing, he must have wondered what was to be his own fate. He had hoped, fervently, that the jewels might be recovered, not simply out of a desire to redeem his own position but out of a genuine concern for the future of the treasures. His removal from office on 23rd October might have accelerated the erosion of his personality and pushed him even further into his fantasy world of psychics and wishful thinking. In fact, it had the opposite effect – it galvanised him. It was as if a weight of uncertainty had finally lifted from his shoulders. Instead of meekly accepting his dismissal, he stayed to have it out with his accusers.

Aberdeen's pious hope that the whole affair would simply go away after the Office of Arms was cleared of its retinue did not come to pass. Instead, initially to save his job and subsequently to save his good name and reputation, Sir Arthur Vicars went on the offensive. He made quite a fight of it too.

6

Whispers

VICARS' RIPOSTE TO his dismissal was swift and pointed. He replied to Dougherty asking if it was 'seriously proposed to dismiss me summarily from my office before an official inquiry has been held as to the loss of the Crown Jewels, and without any evidence that such loss resulted from any neglect or fault on my part'. He insisted that he had guarded the jewels to the best of his ability and as well as he had been permitted. He pointed out that he had asked for a burglar-proof safe from the Board of Works in 1903 and concluded:

> It would be an overwhelming blow to me to be deprived of my official position, after twelve years exemplary service, but to be deprived of it peremptorily, under such circumstances as must leave an impression on the public mind that I had been concerned in, or party to, the removal of the jewels, would be an act of such intolerable and high-handed injustice that I cannot

> *help thinking that His Excellency, the Lord Lieutenant,*
> *and his advisers, would not have taken such a step*
> *unless their minds had been poisoned against me by*
> *false rumours and insinuations of which I know noth-*
> *ing and which upon examination would prove to be*
> *without foundation.*

Vicars' request for an inquiry was swiftly declined by Dougherty and he was told that his office had been 'legally and properly terminated'. Shackleton and Goldney decided not to put up any fight. They were asked for their resignations at the same time as Vicars and they bowed to the inevitable. But the policy decided upon at the 'Star Chamber' meeting of early-October was not implemented in full. Mahony escaped the net completely. He was not even asked to resign his post.

This jeopardised the original consensus of that meeting. The pretext of the reconstitution of the office fell to pieces if Vicars, Shackleton and Goldney were asked to quit and Mahony was allowed to remain in place. This inconsistency was exploited on many subsequent occasions by Vicars and his defenders. Why was it allowed to happen? Probably because of the absence of the redoubtable Sir Anthony MacDonnell, who was still on leave.

In the absence of MacDonnell, Augustine Birrell, his superior, might have been expected to take a greater interest in the fall-out from the theft of the Crown Jewels. One thing that emerges, however, from the correspondence on the subject between October 1907 and January 1908, is that Birrell seemed to pay very little attention to the controversy, even when it was at its height and exercising the minds of his permanent officials. According to Leon O'Broin, his biographer, Birrell 'barely knew of the existence of the Jewels'. In that, he was not unique but, once he did become aware of their existence through their disappearance, he should have paid more heed to the, often labyrinthine, twists in the case.

Unquestionably, he did have other preoccupations. He was attempting to establish his reputation by astute management of the crucial land question and, on the law and order front, he had to deal with the practice of 'cattle driving', an extension of the old Irish tradition of agrarian crime. But Birrell's commitment to the business in hand, whatever it might happen to be, was often suspect. He was undoubtedly talented, yet he achieved little enough in the course of his political career. To the people around him, Birrell appeared to lack application. He was lazy and, on account of this, was often ill informed. Wilfrid Scawen Blunt, in his diaries, mentions that one of Birrell's predecessors as Chief Secretary, George Wyndham, laid the blame for the Crown Jewels fiasco at his door, 'It is Birrell's fault, he… is idle about his work.'

Shortly after Vicars was denied the right to an inquiry, he was accompanied by his solicitor, Mr Meredith, to an interview with Birrell. Reading from a typed document, the Chief Secretary for Ireland listed a number of (according to Vicars) 'trivial charges of negligence, some of which were totally incorrect'. He then informed Vicars that they were the only charges against him and the sole reason for his dismissal.

Sir James Dougherty, the Assistant Under Secretary, filled in for MacDonnell whilst he was on leave. In 1908, he would succeed to the position of Under Secretary on a permanent basis but, as

Assistant Under Secretary, he was neither as assertive as his master nor much given to personal initiatives. In October 1907, he was something of a grey functionary, deputed to correspond with Vicars and his representatives but to follow instructions – given by the Lord Lieutenant, Lord Aberdeen.

The post of Lord Lieutenant was not a position of political power but the Office of Arms, because its officials were answerable only to the King, fell within the Lord Lieutenant's remit. Naturally, the political ramifications of the theft and the ensuing potential scandal meant that Aberdeen needed to have regard to the opinions of his advisers. But, with MacDonnell on leave and Birrell indifferent, Aberdeen began to run the show himself.

He may have appreciated the luxury of being in a position to make decisions, but his handling of the controversy, though well intentioned, was inept. Aberdeen expended much energy on the question between October and December, 1907, and succeeded in antagonising all the interested parties before the storm blew itself out. As he put it himself in his autobiography, 'I cannot recall any individual case to which, during my whole life, I have given so much thought and anxiety as to this.'

Aberdeen allowed his sense of justice and fair play to stand in the way of expediency. It would have been far simpler to clear out the Office of Arms and duck for cover. It would have been unfair to some of the parties concerned, but it would have been uncomplicated as well. Aberdeen, however, lacked MacDonnell's ruthlessness. He hesitated before administering the *coup de grâce*, and the chance was lost. The failure to seek Mahony's resignation, for example, bore all the hallmarks of Aberdeen's impolitic leniency.

Pierce Charles de Lacy O'Mahony, of Grange Con, County Wicklow was a swashbuckling, charismatic figure who had led an adventurous life. Hailing from an old Kerry family, he was about fourteen years older than his half-brother, Sir Arthur Vicars. He had been the nationalist MP for North Meath from 1886 to 1890 and was intensely loyal to the Irish Parliamentary Party leader Charles Stewart Parnell. After the O'Shea divorce case, and the ultimatum to Parnell from the Liberal government, O'Mahony had remained by Parnell's side when the bulk of his colleagues had abandoned him. Just before his death, Parnell had stayed with O'Mahony at the old family home of Kilmorna, County Kerry. Some local anti-Parnellites took the opportunity to make an effigy of Mrs O'Shea and parade it around Kilmorna House for their amusement. After the loss of his seat to the much-revered Michael Davitt in 1890, O'Mahony shifted his attention abroad and became interested in the Balkans, particularly the struggle of the Bulgarians for independence from Turkey. He was visiting Bulgaria when he got news of his half-brother's dismissal and he temporarily abandoned his crusade in the Balkans to take up the cause of his relative.

Forewarned of his arrival and aware of his campaigning qualities, the Irish government made one final 'off the record' effort to persuade Vicars to resign. Meredith, Vicars' solicitor, was summoned to a meeting with Dougherty who swore Meredith to secrecy, not even allowing him to divulge what would pass between them to his client.

The nature of Meredith's meeting was similar to that which

took place around the same time between Augustine Birrell and John Redmond, the leader of the Irish Parliamentary Party. Redmond, an old political ally, had intimated to O'Mahony that he would do all in his power to help Vicars. Birrell, faced with the prospect of a pro-Vicars crusade in Westminster by members of Redmond's party, was wily enough to pre-empt such an awkward campaign. Birrell and Redmond met in late October and discussed the Crown Jewels affair. After the meeting, Redmond's enthusiasm for Vicars' cause had evaporated and his interest was never rekindled. He told O'Mahony about the meeting and proffered a friendly warning: before his old colleague got too engrossed in the defence of his half-brother, Redmond suggested, he should meet Birrell and listen to what he had to say. Birrell had 'conveyed to him the impression that there was something of a grave character behind the accusations of trivial carelessness'. The 'scandalous conduct' card was being played for all it was worth. Dougherty had produced it for Meredith; Birrell had trumped Redmond with it.

Vicars must have expected this strategy from the government. His letter in response to his sacking on 23rd October had referred to minds having been poisoned by 'false rumours and insinuations'. He was aware that tongues were wagging in official circles and that the innuendos circulating about his own character and that of his associates might have been the real basis for his dismissal. He now knew that, although the members of the Irish executive wanted to avoid the publication of the homosexual rumours, they were not above using them, surreptitiously, for their own ends.

In fact, Birrell resorted to the kind of character assassination that was to be employed in the 'Black Diaries' episode in 1916 against Sir Roger Casement. The diaries, graphically illustrating Casement's homosexuality, ended Redmond's involvement in the campaign to have Casement's death sentence commuted. If Redmond, in 1916, withdrew his good offices in a case of life or death, it would have needed far less evidence to convince him to do likewise in 1907. Vicars' life was not at stake, only his livelihood and reputation. Redmond did not want to risk being inveigled into crusading on behalf of a martyr and then have that martyr publicly discredited.

O'Mahony did as Redmond had suggested and met Birrell on 2nd November. Birrell was more candid with the former MP than he had been in his meeting with Vicars; he wasn't expecting to make an ally of O'Mahony, but he was hoping to silence him. Birrell told O'Mahony that the real charge against Vicars was one of 'having associated with a man of undesirable character'. The man in question was Shackleton, Bennett Goldney having already been deemed too peripheral to the activities in Office of Arms to be of further interest. Birrell then issued a vague threat: if Vicars continued to press for a public inquiry, it couldn't be refused, but he suggested that 'in an inquiry of this kind involving character, no matter how innocent a man might be, a certain amount of dirt would stick'. The implication was obvious. If Vicars pressed for an inquiry, the fact of Shackleton's homosexuality and continuing suspicions about his part in the theft would undoubtedly emerge and some of Shackleton's dirt would be bound to stick to Vicars.

O'Mahony defended his half-brother's judgement. Vicars had had no reason to question Shackleton's good character, indeed he had been influenced by the fact that the Dublin Herald was a close friend of Lord Gower, the Duke of Argyll and even the Bishop of Peterborough. What other credentials did a man need? In this, of course, O'Mahony was being disingenuous himself and was meeting bluff with counter bluff. In a public tribunal, Vicars would be certain to mention other acquaintances of Shackleton to whom some traces of dirt might adhere as well. It would not have escaped Birrell's notice that one of those named, the Duke of Argyll, was the King's brother-in-law. When it came to the besmirching of reputations, O'Mahony was hoping that Birrell would opt for a draw.

Birrell's tactics also misfired in another direction. O'Mahony told Birrell that the reasons he had given for rendering a full public inquiry unwise were the very reasons that made an inquiry imperative. In other words, ugly rumours were already being spread about Vicars and he needed a public forum to counter them. Birrell had failed in his primary objective, O'Mahony had not crumbled as easily as Redmond.

At five o'clock that same day, O'Mahony and Birrell met again. This time Aberdeen was present. O'Mahony complained bitterly to Aberdeen that a charge had been laid before the King of Vicars 'associating with an undesirable person'. Birrell protested that Vicars had also been accused of carelessness and that both offences had combined to induce the King to approve of the action that had been taken. This conversation simply reiterated what had already passed between O'Mahony and Birrell. But it does have an importance of its own. The presence of Aberdeen made it more difficult for Birrell to deny O'Mahony's subsequent account of what had been discussed – that something other than Vicars' alleged carelessness had prompted the Irish administration to sack him and that he was being victimised because of his association with Shackleton. Later, through MacDonnell, Birrell did insist that O'Mahony's report of the conversation was 'quite inaccurate', but Aberdeen never attempted to cast doubt on O'Mahony's version of events, though he was challenged to do so.

Politics are peripheral to the Crown Jewels affair, even though many of those involved were politicians or public servants. But it is odd, nonetheless, to find an old-style nationalist (O'Mahony) lining up alongside a unionist (Vicars) to take on a Liberal administration in which his principal opponent (MacDonnell) was a man with strong nationalist sympathies. These alliances, of course, had more to do with family ties and self-interest than politics.

O'Mahony, despite the fact that he was campaigning on behalf of an inveterate loyalist in Sir Arthur Vicars, played his nationalist political contacts for all they were worth. In the short-term, he was to use Joe O'Beirne, an old Parnellite and former member of the extremist Irish Republican Brotherhood. In the longer term, as we have seen, he would enlist the support of the Irish Parliamentary Party's maverick MP, Laurence Ginnell.

O'Beirne was manager of *The Peasant*, a newspaper to which Bulmer Hobson was a contributor. Hobson, like O'Beirne, was a former IRB man. He was an associate of Arthur Griffith, the founder of Sinn Féin, and was also involved in the newspaper

The Republic. Hobson had become professionally and politically interested in the theft of the Crown Jewels, sensing that there might be some political capital to be made out of it.

When approached by O'Beirne, O'Mahony displayed no reluctance to talk about the affair. He invited Hobson and O'Beirne to visit him at his Grange Con home. What he told them (repeated by Hobson in his book *Ireland, Yesterday and Tomorrow*), was astounding. His story, for the first time, puts Vicars' belief in Shackleton's guilt into some kind of perspective. O'Mahony had cross-examined Vicars thoroughly about the goings-on at the Office of Arms. He had jettisoned the utterly fantastic, accepted the plausible and offered Hobson and O'Beirne a thesis that cannot be dismissed lightly.

O'Mahony told Hobson and O'Beirne that two men had been responsible for the theft of the Crown Jewels. One was Shackleton, the other was a friend of his – an exotic, violent and plausible rogue, Captain Richard Howard Gorges. Gorges, according to O'Mahony, had actually stolen the jewels while Shackleton had provided him with the appropriate keys. When the crime was committed, Shackleton was safely in England working on his alibi, his presence there being corroborated by some of his well-placed friends and associates.

Gorges was a volatile and unpredictable character. He came from an old Anglo-Irish family that was no longer genteel or prosperous. The family had come over to Ireland in Cromwell's time and the succeeding generations had continued in the service of the crown. Richard Howard Gorges was the ranking black sheep of the family. Accounts of his life are a mixture of verifiable truth and unsupported anecdote, the excesses evident in the verifiable lending considerable credence to the anecdotal. Putting fact and rumour together, a picture emerges of an unpleasant, belligerent rake, possessed of sufficient charm to endear him to some and enough animal courage to earn the respect of others. In both cases, his admirers would normally have been members of his own sex – not many women seemed to wander into his orbit.

In the 1870s, he had spent his youth in Kingstown (Dún Laoghaire) where his aggression made him unpopular amongst his neighbours. At the age of fourteen, this aggression had been channelled in a useful direction when he joined the army. There is a story that he was forced to leave the town in a hurry when he was suspected of molesting small girls. Given his relative youth, and his subsequent sexual preferences, the story is likely to be apocryphal. His military career took him to South Africa where he served with the Cape Mounted Police. He went on to serve in the Matabele War in 1896 where he succumbed to severe sun-stroke, as a consequence of which he began to suffer from intense headaches, something that didn't help his already morbid disposition. He began to drink too much to ease the frequent pain, with predictable results.

During the Boer War, he fought with the 9th Border Regiment, was wounded at least three times and earned two medals and many commendations for courage. War was not a problem for Richard Howard Gorges. Living with the prospect of a quick and violent death gave him an excuse for irrational, belligerent behaviour, frequent bouts of black depression and a multitude of excesses. That kind of conduct was no easier to control in peacetime, but was more difficult to justify.

After the end of the Boer War in 1902, Gorges became a

regimental musketry instructor, based in Portsmouth but with responsibility for militia training. He was to find himself back in Ireland on a regular basis for militia training exercises. On one of his stays, he either met or renewed an acquaintance with Shackleton. Despite their different backgrounds, they had a lot in common – both had served in South Africa, they were also self-indulgent, profligate *bon viveurs* and both were homosexual. As Hobson puts it, 'It was the conjunction of the black sheep of the Shackletons and the black sheep of the Gorges' that set things moving in Dublin Castle.'

During his meeting with O'Beirne and Hobson, O'Mahony passed on information dragged from a reluctant Vicars about the drinks parties in the Office of Arms. It comes as no surprise to learn, from what he told the two journalists, that Vicars' capacity for drink was limited. He was capable of holding one or two sherries before his interest in proceedings ended. According to O'Mahony, Lord Haddo also made a habit of attending these functions. One night, after Vicars had passed his limit and was in supine and blissful slumber, Haddo had taken the bunch of keys from Vicars' pocket, opened the safe and made off with the Crown Jewels. He returned them to their distraught guardian the next day.

The story may seem incredible but, when taken in conjunction with some other imponderables, it becomes more cohesive and convincing. It might explain the presence of Haddo in the Office of Arms early in 1907 when Mrs Farrell stumbled across him. This is not to suggest that he was actually returning the jewels at the time, but the practical joke and his unwarranted appearance might have been connected.

It also helps to account for Vicars' apparent conviction that the jewels would be restored to his custody. On Monday 8th July, he had told Kerr that he wouldn't be surprised to find them returned by parcel post. Haddo was not in the country at the time, he was out of Ireland from March to November of 1907, but Vicars obviously hoped that someone else was playing an equally tasteless practical joke.

In this context, one wonders if the police would have been notified of the theft of the jewels on 6th July had Vicars not sent Stivey to the safe instead of going himself? Would he first have put the word about amongst his associates that the joke had gone too far this time and that the jewels must be returned? Or was his unprecedented decision to give the safe key to Stivey the action of a man who already knew the jewels were missing? By 6th July had Vicars begun to give up hope that the theft was a mere prank, realised that the 'discovery' of the loss would have to be expedited but preferred that the alarm be raised by somebody else?

According to Hobson, O'Mahony told him that Shackleton and Gorges had been present when Haddo had played his sadistic trick on Vicars. It had dawned on both, O'Mahony speculated, just how insecure the jewels were. And both Shackleton and Gorges needed money: Shackleton's long-term investments, upon which he based his hopes of future prosperity, would only pay off if huge sums were injected periodically to prime the pump; and Gorges was perennially hard up and sufficiently amoral to be unconcerned about how he might come by a large sum of money.

Between them, insisted O'Mahony, they had concocted a plan to steal the jewels. Shackleton was smart enough to realise that his financial situation and his access to Vicars would make him a prime suspect. The annual militia training took place in June and July every year. Gorges would be in Dublin on legitimate business for a month. Shackleton took himself elsewhere. Gorges was a familiar figure in Dublin Castle, his movements would arouse minimal interest. He also possessed the requisite daring to carry out the theft. The jewels, O'Mahony and Vicars theorised, had then been taken, by Shackleton, to Amsterdam, the 'gem capital' of Europe, where they had been pawned.

The story didn't end there. According to O'Mahony, the police had quickly realised who the criminals were by connecting Shackleton to Gorges. The two men were questioned and it was from this police interrogation that the Dublin Castle authorities became aware of the homosexual scandal and the Office of Arms soirees. O'Mahony claimed 'they dared the authorities to arrest them and said that, if they were arrested, they would uncover so many scandals that they would shake the government'. When names such as Lord Gower and the Duke of Argyll were mentioned in relation to Shackleton, the police had begun to back off and had passed the case back to their political superiors. Vicars was being victimised to protect two blackmailers and their potential victims.

O'Mahony's conversation with Hobson and O'Beirne had the desired effect. The two journalists had not been given the story in confidence, they were expected to use it without, of course, naming the source. As you might expect, however, nobody would touch it, the potential for libel actions was limitless. Eventually, Hobson's colourful version of O'Mahony's story found its way into the New York *Gaelic American* newspaper edited by the old Fenian, John Devoy – but even the virulently anti-British Devoy, relatively secure against defamation suits in the US, felt the need to amend and modify it.

Word of mouth, however, was a different matter. Hobson and O'Beirne happily regaled others with O'Mahony's version of events. The story satisfied a need amongst Dublin nationalists and republicans to believe that the Castle was a den of iniquity and vice as well as a source of political repression.

While O'Mahony was countering the treatment being meted out to Vicars by the castle, Aberdeen was beginning to waver. He was a fair man who believed in natural justice while the country's leading civil servant, the Under Secretary Sir Anthony MacDonnell (nicknamed the 'Bengal Tiger'), was more of a pragmatist who tended towards the expedient. However, MacDonnell was on vacation through most of November 1907. With MacDonnell away, Aberdeen could give rein to the compassionate side of his character. In addition to his innate sense of fair play, however, Aberdeen was also concerned about O'Mahony's potential for raising embarrassing hares and the possible consequences if he continued this sport unchecked. Aberdeen was gravitating towards a breaking of ranks. On 5th November, he wrote to Knollys: 'My feeling is that while, on the one hand absolute firmness is necessary, care should be taken at the same time to avoid any step or attitude which might hereafter have the semblance of an unwillingness to allow any person concerned, to make a defence.' Aberdeen was dithering.

He told Knollys that O'Mahony had threatened to enlist the aid of MPs in asking questions at Westminster. However, O'Mahony had done much more. He had engaged the services of the eminent barrister James H Campbell (a future Lord Chief Justice of Ireland) on behalf of Vicars. He had also written to Birrell's office formally accusing the Irish government of having trumped up charges of negligence against his half-brother when the real charge (which had been laid before the King) was one of 'having introduced into the Office of Arms, and shared his own house with, a person of undesirable character'. He demanded to see the 'document' that had been laid before the King containing these charges, insisting that Vicars could not defend himself until he knew exactly what he stood accused of. He concluded by reproaching the administration for the attempt to suborn Meredith, who had been sworn to secrecy by Dougherty. 'But the object of the interview,' railed O'Mahony, 'was to persuade him to advise my brother to send in his resignation and that before I had time to arrive in Dublin.'

This vitriolic broadside was O'Mahony's formal declaration of war on behalf of his half-brother. Vicars' complaints were now on record if not actually public. However, O'Mahony's move was a calculated risk. It put pressure on the government and might have caused them to relent (as Aberdeen had done) but it might also have created a siege mentality and have led to a hardening of attitudes. More overt pressure could be exerted by a series of parliamentary questions. But here time was not on his side. O'Mahony would not be able to prime and organise such a campaign before the new session of parliament in early 1908. It took time to brief selected parliamentary 'bushwhackers' and to get the questions on the list. So, in the interim, O'Mahony turned to the Knights of St Patrick. He took the unprecedented step of composing a petition that he asked the knights to sign. It was addressed to the King, cited Vicars' excellent service and requested 'that an inquiry into all the circumstances connected with the recent disappearance of the Insignia of the Order, at which Ulster [Vicars] may be given an opportunity of being heard before any steps be taken to relieve him from his office, would be only fair and just'.

Of the twenty-one knights, sixteen signed. Of the remainder, one was out of the country, one was ill and three refused to have anything to do with the petition. One of the latter, Lord Iveagh, pointed out in his response, 'I happen to have been told by Lord Knollys that the presentation of this petition would be distasteful to the King.' He could not have been more right. Lord Kilmorey, another knight who did not sign, was the King's Aide-de-Camp, he too sounded a note of warning, 'From what I have heard I think it much better that the Knights should not approach the King by petition.'

The hints were heavy, but they were ignored and the petition was presented. Ultimately, the stand of Iveagh and Kilmorey was amply vindicated. Those responsible for the petition should have had some presentiment of this when, on 15th November 1907, Field Marshall Earl Roberts, one of the sixteen who had signed, sent a telegram from Windsor asking that his name be withdrawn from it.

With the uncompromising Sir Anthony MacDonnell still on leave in late November 1907, Aberdeen devised a new line of attack to circumvent the impasse created by the utter refusal of Vicars to go quietly. The first prong of this strategy was the introduction of an outside arbitrator. Aberdeen proposed to Knollys an approach to a former Master of the Rolls, Sir Alexander Porter. He was to be asked for a dispassionate opinion on the whole affair once the facts were presented to him.

Knollys' reply to this suggestion, sent on 23rd November, merits quotation in full.

> *I have submitted to the King your letter of the 21st and he approves of the suggestion that an arbitrator, in the person of Sir Alexander Porter, should be appointed to enquire into Sir Arthur Vicars' case.*
>
> *Perhaps you would kindly let me know if he is (1) to enquire into the statements relating to Sir Arthur Vicars' complicity in abnormal practices; or (2) into the charges of alleged carelessness in his custody of the Crown Jewels; or (3) both. As regards the first I imagine it is pretty well proved that he was an intimate friend of one if not two men about whose guilt there is no more doubt, but to prove more in an inquiry such as is proposed, would be, I believe, an impossibility even if he is guilty.*

> [The 'guilt' in question was not a reference to the theft but to homosexuality.]

Porter was deputed to examine both the issue of 'abnormal practices' and that of negligence in the care of the jewels. His conclusions are important because, over a concentrated period of time, he spoke to all the major players. At a distance of almost a century, it is difficult to decide if Vicars was being fairly or harshly treated by the Castle authorities. Porter's judgement was about the only contemporary disinterested opinion expressed on the matter. His confidential statement confirmed the view of the administration that Vicars was primarily responsible for the loss of the insignia. As regards his associations, Porter was unconvinced by charges that Vicars was homosexual. The case was not proven and he was entitled to the presumption of innocence. He did, however, say that Vicars had been 'very unfortunate in some of his acquaintances'.

Aberdeen outlined a new course of action on foot of Porter's report. Vicars would be asked, once again, to resign 'on the understanding that he will be reappointed for heraldic functions only'. This meant, in effect, that he would become a full-time genealogist. A new official would be appointed to administer the Office of Arms, who would also be designated Registrar of the Order of St Patrick. His salary would be deducted from that currently drawn by Vicars. That was a major flaw in the proposed arrangement as far as Sir Arthur was concerned – he was not a wealthy man and his salary was important to him.

On the same day that Aberdeen advanced his own strategy with this new set of proposals, he was presented with the petition from the fifteen Knights of St Patrick requesting an inquiry into the theft of the Crown Jewels. It was clear that Aberdeen, as Grand Master of the Order, was expected to transmit the petition to the King, who was the only person who could order such an inquiry. However, this request was not stated overtly in the petition. Aberdeen, knowing what the King's reaction would be and, fearing the effect the King's anger would have on the *démarche* that he was proposing, decided to sit on the document until the deal he had cobbled together had been accepted and the petition was no longer relevant.

As far as he was concerned, the petition 'has merely been placed in my hands informally, partly by way of information'. Unfortunately for Aberdeen and his elaborate plans, at this point Sir Anthony MacDonnell's four weeks of leave expired and he returned to Dublin. Within days, the fragile edifice of compromise that Aberdeen had carefully constructed came crashing to the ground.

Prior to Vicars' refusal to resign, the sordid whisperings about him and the Office of Arms had been relatively desultory and completely disorganised. It was less a case of government-inspired character assassination than of those in the know being unable to resist a bit of gossip. Birrell's attempts to 'seduce' Redmond and O'Mahony brought the campaign to a different level of intent without introducing very much sophistication. But it was not until the return to Dublin of Sir Anthony MacDonnell that anything resembling an actual smear campaign can be said to have begun in earnest.

When MacDonnell returned to work in late November 1907, he discovered that Vicars was still in office, refusing to budge, and that Aberdeen was attempting to accommodate him. MacDonnell determined immediately to, as he put it himself, 'bring the case back to the point it had reached before I went on leave'. Having reached his decision to be rid of Vicars, he never wavered.

Sir Anthony MacDonnell, sixty-three years old at the time of the Crown Jewels affair, was a forceful, almost aggressive, personality, both opinionated and acerbic. He was a Catholic, Liberal by inclination and even had a brother in the Irish Parliamentary Party. His dynamism and vigour led to frequent differences of opinion with the less engaged Chief Secretary Augustine Birrell. It was one of their rows that would lead to MacDonnell's resignation in 1908 and his replacement by Sir James Dougherty. All in all, he was a man to suffer neither carelessness nor inefficiency gladly – and he considered Vicars guilty of both. Neither would he have had much time for Vicars' brand of unionism.

There is no doubt that MacDonnell genuinely believed that Sir Arthur's negligence alone merited dismissal. The allegations of 'scandalous conduct' in the Office of Arms merely added to the urgency of the total purge that had been envisaged at the end of October and then reneged upon. As far as MacDonnell was concerned, a major scandal would have diverted attention away from the real issues of the day. But how far was he prepared to go to persuade Vicars that his best interests lay in going quickly and going quietly? Did he use the power of his office to smear Vicars? It might have occurred to MacDonnell that cranking up the rumour mill would put pressure on Vicars and help him to come to the 'right' decision. It is impossible to document such a claim but it is not hard to accept historian Leon O'Broin's assertion that MacDonnell circulated a report 'that there was a connection between Vicars and a group of homosexuals in London'.

Whatever unsanctioned actions MacDonnell might have employed to get rid of Vicars, he had one huge advantage in his official campaign to secure Sir Arthur's dismissal – he was highly respected by King Edward VII. The King was influenced in his regard for the Irishman by Knollys, who was a personal friend of MacDonnell. Both the King and Knollys tended to accept MacDonnell's view of Irish affairs. Aberdeen had been appointed to advise the King on such matters, but Edward VII disliked him and considered him to lack both dignity and acumen.

MacDonnell was appalled by what he found on his return to Dublin at the end of November. He reacted angrily to Vicars' refusal to go quietly. He dashed off a letter to Knollys designed to circumvent the negotiations being carried on by Aberdeen. He had no qualms about going over Aberdeen's head.

MacDonnell had been told of Porter's confidential examination of Vicars' guilt. He was not impressed. As far as he was concerned, Porter's conclusions were no different from those that had already prompted the Irish executive to sack the man. Porter had confirmed Vicars' negligence and had given him the benefit of the doubt when it came to the homosexual aspect of the case. To MacDonnell's way of thinking, none of this justified Vicars' retention.

MacDonnell also played on the King's recently acquired dislike for Vicars. Edward VII had issued instructions that Vicars would never again be allowed in his presence 'either officially or privately'. MacDonnell reminded Knollys that Vicars, under the new arrangement devised by Aberdeen, would still, as an officer of the Order of St Patrick, be entitled to attend official functions. The King would, from time to time, be present on such occasions. Encounters would be unavoidable.

MacDonnell pointed out that rumours of the scandal were widespread by now (a fact he was well aware of as he was probably assiduously spreading them himself). He reinforced his case by emphasising that the failure to fire Vicars would cause renewed suspicion and speculation, particularly after the dismissal of Shackleton and Goldney. He suggested that it was time the King distanced himself from the affair, washed his hands of the matter entirely and left it to the Irish government to settle. This would, of course, mean delegating authority to MacDonnell to do as he saw fit.

King Edward was only too glad to let MacDonnell take up the running. Knollys was instructed to write to Aberdeen and dash his hopes of extracting some kind of deal for Vicars. Crucially, however, the King insisted that Vicars was to be dismissed purely on the grounds of carelessness. Although MacDonnell had triumphed in the bureaucratic battle, it was left to poor Aberdeen to administer the decision. It was not an easy letter for him to write. He had to tell Vicars that his efforts at compromise had failed and that he would not be allowed to occupy a modified position in the Office of Arms. The administration was reverting to its stance of 23rd October. The Office of Arms was being reconstituted and Vicars' services were no longer required. Furthermore, he was told that his dismissal was solely on account of the loss of the insignia. He was given an ultimatum. If he did not resign by Monday 9th December (the letter was sent on 7th December) he would be dismissed. With all hope of agreement at an end, hostilities now commenced in earnest.

Instead of a letter of resignation, Aberdeen got a long, detailed reply from O'Mahony that went over familiar ground. O'Mahony had gone to the trouble to write such a comprehensive letter for two reasons. Firstly, there was a stated threat of the publication of its contents if satisfaction was not forthcoming. Secondly, a copy was sent to the Home Secretary, Herbert Gladstone. In the letter, O'Mahony accused the government of concealing the real charge against Vicars, namely that of having introduced a man of 'undesirable character' into the Office of Arms. O'Mahony doesn't mention Shackleton by name, but refers to his association with Lord Gower and the Duke of Argyll. He scoffed at the attempt of the administration to modify, retrospectively, the charge against Vicars to one of negligence. It was too late for that, the 'incontinence of official tongues' had already done its work.

O'Mahony also had something more concrete to offer than mere rhetoric. The 1905 Statutes of the Order of St Patrick had been formulated by Vicars. According to O'Mahony not even the King had the right to get rid of Ulster King of Arms (Vicars) because he held his post 'during good behaviour'. So, contended O'Mahony, it all came down to a question of what constituted 'good behaviour' and the term could only be properly defined, he maintained, by an official inquiry.

In his initial response to the ultimatum from the Irish executive, O'Mahony had held off from expressing his true opinion, though he had hinted at it. His view was that Vicars was only a ritual scapegoat. He was being sacrificed to protect others, particularly the well-connected Shackleton. However, on 9th December, the day on which Vicars was due to jump or be pushed, he put that view on the record. He wrote again to Aberdeen making just such a claim. He mentioned no names. He knew he didn't need to.

Herbert Gladstone entered the picture on 11th December 1907. O'Mahony, still in pursuit of an inquiry, was making no progress in Dublin, so he decided to outflank the Irish executive and enlist some help in London. It was his final throw of the dice.

Gladstone was an obvious choice for defender of the underdog. As Home Secretary, he was, except for Birrell, the cabinet member with most involvement in Irish affairs. He was also the son of the great Liberal Prime Minister, William Ewart Gladstone, Ireland's great British champion of the 19th century. However, Herbert Gladstone was not the force the 'Grand Old Man' had been. Neither did his interest in Ireland approach that of his father. But he was a fair-minded man who could view the Crown Jewels affair dispassionately.

O'Mahony adopted a temperate approach to Gladstone. He avoided any of the virulence that had already been generated by the controversy, reasoning that this would instantly scare Gladstone off. He simply wrote to Gladstone and informed him that Vicars had been fired, repeated his point about the terms under which Vicars had held his position and asked for an inquiry. Three days later, O'Mahony discovered that the petition of the Knights of St Patrick had not been presented to the King as there had been no formal request to do so. This provoked him into a more aggressive response.

On 16th December, O'Mahony sent a second, more indignant letter to Gladstone. In it, he upbraided Aberdeen for doing nothing with the petition and asked Gladstone to pass it on to the King. Gladstone was unaware of Aberdeen's motives in keeping the petition to himself and, not being at all *au fait* with the King's probable reaction to the document, obligingly did as he was asked. Thus, unwittingly, did he enter the Crown Jewels maze. However, once he realised where he was he extricated himself from it at the earliest possible moment.

The first piece of correspondence from Gladstone to Aberdeen, sent on 18th December, was a transparent reprimand of the Lord Lieutenant. He ridiculed Aberdeen's pretext for withholding the petition and reminded him that when loyal subjects signed a petition addressed to the King, it was a safe bet that they expected it to be presented. It was not for Aberdeen's eyes only and Gladstone intended to submit the document. The question he posed in the letter to Aberdeen was what recommendation should he make? Should he counsel the King to comply with the request for an inquiry or should he advise the opposite? Did O'Mahony's claim that Vicars could not be sacked have any validity? For his own part, Gladstone insisted he had no doubt about Vicars' negligence, but felt the charges of immorality necessitated a tribunal of some kind in which Sir Arthur, if innocent, could clear his name.

Gladstone was also aware that the new session of parliament was imminent and that Irish nationalists would wish to capitalise on any mishandling of the affair. They would, in a unique mis-alliance, find themselves bedded down with unionists on the issue. The unionists had no love for a Liberal Irish administration and considered some of its chief civil servants to be rabid nationalists. It would be a pleasure for them to inflict embarrassment and discomfort on Sir Anthony MacDonnell. Furthermore, Vicars was one of their own.

Piqued by the criticism implied in Gladstone's letter, Aberdeen responded the following day (19th December) with one of his own, a hymn of self-justification worthy of Vicars himself. After making numerous excuses (some legitimate) for the conduct of the case so far, he informed Gladstone that the decision to jettison Vicars had the approval of the King and sound legal advice was that Vicars could be sacked.

Gladstone decided to venture just a little further into the maze. Here his innate politician's instinct for self-preservation was letting him down. Inspector Kane was sent for. The story he related convinced Gladstone that Vicars was already teetering on the brink due to the weakness of his position and it only remained for the final push to be administered. An inquiry would provide the necessary propulsion and bring the entire debacle to a swift, if somewhat unsatisfactory, conclusion. Gladstone made up his mind.

On the 21st December, Gladstone sent a telegram to O'Mahony informing him that the petition of the Knights of St Patrick was on its way to Edward VII and that approval for a royal commission of inquiry was being sought. From Gladstone's private papers, it is clear that he saw this commission as a 'hanging jury'. But he would still be able to give O'Mahony exactly what he wanted. Gladstone proceeded on the assumption that the King's consent for a royal commission was a matter of course. Speed was imperative. Gladstone wanted the inquiry over and the recommendations known before the new session of parliament began early in the New Year.

As to the scope of the commission, Gladstone and Aberdeen were agreed that it would be limited only to the theft of the jewels. Nothing was to be allowed interfere with a quick, clean and decisive finding against Vicars. On 26th December, Prime Minister Campbell-Bannerman gave his approval for the appointment of a royal commission, with three members, to inquire into the circumstances of the disappearance of the jewels. But they had not reckoned on the bloody-mindedness of the King. Incensed by the knights' petition, he obdurately refused to countenance a royal commission. As the King was the only person entitled to appoint a royal commission, his consent was essential. Gladstone, therefore, was kindly to advise the petitioners that their petition had not been granted.

Like Aberdeen before him, Gladstone watched his carefully crafted scheme fall to pieces. His reply, however, was a model of tact. Anything less than a royal commission would be unlikely to attract the sort of influential commissioners whose decisions would satisfy parliament. The only other apparent option was a departmental tribunal, held at civil-service level. The spectacle of the Irish government dutifully investigating itself would please certain nationalist and unionist elements immensely. They would tear into such a procedure right from the start of the new session.

Gladstone tried rational argument with the King. He pointed out that a departmental tribunal was hardly the place to investigate a serious crime. Anything less than a royal commission would mean that testimony could not be taken on oath. Witnesses might make libellous suggestions and both they, and the commissioners, would be liable to be sued. Furthermore, the members of the Irish executive would be vulnerable to accusations of a cover-up if they employed their own to investigate their own. Sound arguments all. They might have swayed an open mind, but Edward VII wasn't listening.

It was Aberdeen who solved the problem. He put forward the idea of a viceregal commission, a tribunal that he himself (as

Viceroy) had the power to appoint. It would be an independent outside agency and, theoretically, free from any taint of partiality. As long as the commissioners had legal protection, the right men could be found to serve. There were, however, disadvantages. Evidence could not be taken on oath, neither could witnesses be compelled to attend or testify. However, Gladstone didn't want it right, he wanted it now, so it was decided that a viceregal commission was the best option.

Two co-operative Irishmen had already been found to officiate. They were Judge James Johnston Shaw KC, who would be Chairman, and Mr Robert Fitzwilliam Starkie. Both had agreed to participate on the understanding that they would be serving on a royal commission. Shaw was tempted by the fact that, informally at least, the commission would bear his name. But, loyally, when he discovered that he was not to chair a royal commission, he swallowed his disappointment and overcame his misgivings. Starkie did likewise. All that was missing now was a third commissioner.

Both Gladstone and Aberdeen were inclined to hurry the entire procedure along though for different reasons. Gladstone wanted to head off the inevitable parliamentary ambush; Aberdeen was aware that the Castle season was approaching. Vicars was always an integral part of the festivities and events. Now that his departure was merely a matter of form, Aberdeen wished him gone as soon as possible. So the inquiry was set in motion with startling rapidity. Barely a week elapsed before the commissioners were sitting in the library of the Office of Arms across from Sir Arthur Vicars and his representatives.

The third commissioner was English, a Mr Chester Jones who

was there for a single reason, to keep an eye on things for Gladstone, who still retained a proprietorial interest in the inquiry.

But, within the precincts of Dublin Castle, not even Herbert Gladstone was the true proprietor.

Sir Anthony MacDonnell was profoundly unhappy with the course of events. He had abandoned a position of power in India to become an adviser to the Irish government, yet his superiors seemed hellbent on ignoring, or improving upon, his advice.

The Crown Jewels affair had dragged on for six months since July 1907. MacDonnell was, instinctively, an impatient man. His approach to the problem had been consistent all along; consistent and ruthless. He had long since decided that Vicars was sloppy, absentminded and careless and that, due to his incompetence, a valuable and symbolic jewel collection had been rifled and, therefore, he should be dismissed. It was a stark and brutal equation that was typical of MacDonnell's mentality.

MacDonnell would have been livid at any intimation that he was being unfair to Vicars. As far as he was concerned, the man was merely getting his deserts. Not even Herbert Gladstone disputed this. The dismissal of Vicars was the only way in which justice could be done. Unfortunately for MacDonnell, Gladstone had an old-fashioned and sentimental attachment to the idea that justice should be seen to be done as well. Gladstone would not be perturbed were Vicars to be found guilty of negligence, but he was uncomfortable with the knowledge that the man had been tried, convicted and sentenced, *in absentia* and in secret.

But the intervention of Gladstone was inconvenient for MacDonnell. When it came to the Crown Jewels, MacDonnell's lead was followed by Birrell, who was eminently biddable and tractable on the subject, primarily because, when he paid it the least attention, he was frankly baffled by the whole affair.

Gladstone's interest, however, was tougher for MacDonnell to deal with because he filled the vacuum left by Birrell's indifference. MacDonnell had no choice but to defer to the Home Secretary's wishes. Having, so he thought, already settled the matter, MacDonnell must have been irritated by the turn of events. There was no way around an instruction from Gladstone that a viceregal commission was to be established. But MacDonnell had enough confidence in his own bureaucratic talents to believe that the potential damage could be limited.

Once MacDonnell could no longer avoid a viceregal commission, he changed his strategy. A warrant had been issued instructing him to establish such a body, but its wording had been vague. It suited him to make no attempt to clarify the terms of reference with the Home Office and so he was left with considerable room for manoeuvre. The warrant did not specify whether the tribunal was to be public or private. In addition, the terms of reference of the commission could be interpreted in the narrowest possible way. It was being established to inquire into the circumstances of the loss of the regalia but, more specifically, into 'whether Sir Arthur Vicars exercised due vigilance and proper care as the custodian thereof'.

MacDonnell decided that total secrecy was out of the question. It was a viceregal commission that would issue a report and that might choose to publish testimony. But, while it was in session, he was determined to ensure that the press and other interested parties were excluded. Vicars would be permitted legal representation and some of his supporters would be admitted as observers. That was publicity enough for MacDonnell. His manipulation was really quite audacious, but he was sufficiently confident in his own position to flout certain conventions. It was an understood thing that viceregal commissions were conducted in public. Equally, it was customary, when a permanent official was in any doubt about the execution of an order, for him to consult the person who had given the order. MacDonnell resolutely refused to be shackled by either convention because, in this instance, neither suited his purpose.

In advance of the arrival of Chester Jones, the third member of the commission, Shaw and Starkie were told the wishes of the Irish government and were happy to comply. The press and general public would not be admitted, it would have been difficult to find room for them anyway. The commission was set to convene in the library of the Office of Arms, in surroundings that were intimate but cramped. The choice of venue meant that there was little room for reporters. MacDonnell had made sure of that. Chester Jones arrived in Dublin on Thursday 9th January 1908 and settled into the Shelbourne Hotel. Shortly afterwards, he kept an appointment to meet his fellow commissioners.

Jones, of course, had been selected by Gladstone to ensure that the business was handled properly; in other words exactly as Gladstone wanted it to be handled. He did not know the two men who were to sit with him on the commission nor the key players in the machinations that had led to his presence in Dublin. Jones was a visitor, a stranger and an interloper.

If he was hoping to be put at his ease by Shaw and Starkie at their first meeting, then he was disappointed. The two Irishmen were polite, but they were also businesslike and distant. Decisions had already been taken before his arrival and they intended to stick to them, with or without his consent. On the question of privacy, Jones was dumbfounded to learn that the press and public were to be excluded from the hearings. He protested but was duly voted down. MacDonnell had got his way.

Act Two

The Scapegoat

7

The Commission Sits

'The Irish Government [has] been pecking in private at this matter for some months.'

Herbert Gladstone to Augustine Birrell, 13th January 1908

THE SETTING FOR the confrontation between Vicars and his accusers was suitably modest – the library of the Office of Arms, Dublin Castle. More exalted impeachment proceedings in the past had taken place in the House of Lords in London, but this was a squalid little affair and the cramped library was a fitting venue. It is not often that a commission sits at the very scene of the crime.

The long table in the middle of the library had been removed for the occasion and a blazing coal fire took the winter chill from the room. The safe had not been moved, it still stood in its corner. It was not there as a mute, ironic reminder to all concerned, there was simply nowhere else to put it and it would be needed in the course of the inquiry.

The three commissioners sat on the same side of the room as the safe. To their left were a few seats for counsel and the carefully vetted observers. In front of them was a chair for the witnesses. Upstairs, the work of the Office of Arms went on. The staff considered the inquiry a nuisance because the library was off limits for its duration – except when they, themselves, were called as witnesses. Each day that the commission continued, the work upstairs would grind to a halt as it was discovered that an essential research book was nestling in a cabinet somewhere in the library.

At eleven o'clock on that Friday morning, the room was crowded. The three commissioners – Shaw, Starkie and Jones – were seated behind a table. To one side of them was the Solicitor General, Redmond Barry, the man who, ultimately, would be questioning the witnesses. On the other side sat Mr C T Beard, Secretary to the Commission, and a shorthand writer, pencil poised, ready to record the evidence.

Outside the Bedford Tower was a group of reporters, trying to keep warm while they waited to be allowed in.

Vicars was the only witness in the room. He was accompanied by Meredith, his solicitor, and was represented by two of Ireland's most distinguished barristers: James H Campbell and Timothy Healy. Campbell he had consulted before, but the gruff and pugnacious Timothy Healy he had not.

Healy's presence was clear evidence that Pierce O'Mahony had put his half-brother's defence before his own personal feelings. At the time of the Nationalist Party split over Parnell, Healy had been a rabid anti-Parnellite. He had savaged his former leader in a manner that went well beyond the limits of acceptable political virulence. In the intervening years, when others attempted to heal the wounds caused by the split, Healy had established himself as the country's foremost political maverick. Although it was paradoxical of O'Mahony to choose, as one of Vicars' representatives, a man who had tormented his beloved Parnell, he was conscious of the credibility Healy's presence would give Vicars' cause. Healy's unparalleled gift for ridicule and invective meant he was a good man to have on your side and a perfect foil for the less flamboyant, but highly methodical, James Campbell.

Both men were waiting to pounce. As soon as Beard had finished reading out the warrant, Campbell was on his feet. He didn't bother with any deferential preliminaries or niceties. The conspicuous absence of any members of the public probably answered his question before he even asked it. He addressed the Chairman, Judge Shaw, 'I wish to be informed sir, by you, at the outset, whether it is intended to conduct these proceedings in public or in private?'

'Well, the intention,' replied Shaw, 'I think, was to conduct the proceedings in private, but we are ready to hear any application that may be made as to that.'

'Am I right, also, sir,' Campbell continued, 'in the belief that we entertain, that under the Warrant appointing you, you have no power to compel the attendance of witnesses and no power to examine witnesses on oath?'

'Well,' the judge admitted, 'I understand that that is so.'

It had taken Campbell only a few seconds to expose the commission's soft underbelly. He then went on to assert that Vicars would never take part in a private inquiry. He wanted a public forum in which to refute the stories and rumours 'of a grave character' being circulated about him, particularly as this innuendo had been communicated to the King. But Campbell wasn't merely objecting to the privacy of the commission, he totally rejected its terms of reference too. It was going to be a one-sided affair, delving into the facts of the theft only insofar as they related to Vicars' negligence. Shaw made no attempt to contradict him. The Chairman was quite emphatic on this point as well. He would make no concession on the scope of the inquiry, even though it was becoming apparent that Campbell was about to walk out and take the main focus of the investigation with him.

Campbell had not expected Shaw to budge on this issue. His opening questions show that he knew what to expect from the inquiry. Vicars' representatives had no real intention of taking part in the proceedings. They had come along to confirm their suspicions, to withdraw from the inquiry and to be first into the courtyard outside the Bedford Tower to meet and talk to the press. In an era much less accustomed to media management, they had even brought prepared statements with them. They knew they would probably be leaving early.

Campbell, in his matter-of-fact fashion, addressed Shaw. 'I can only say, speaking on behalf of Sir Arthur Vicars, that he will decline to take any part whatever in such an investigation. It is a partial one. It is an investigation into a matter upon which the executive have already made up their minds, because they have told him so over and over again… and what concerns him more than anything is the charge *not* formulated… the matters of insinuation against his personal character.'

Campbell didn't even bother to make a formal application for a full, public, sworn inquiry. He knew it was not in the power of the commission to grant that request. Those in a position to make such a concession were unwilling to do so. Vicars and his representatives then formally withdrew from the inquiry that they had fought for months to have established. Campbell motioned to Healy who rose from his chair. Both men made a suitably deferential gesture towards the commissioners and walked out of the room, closely followed by Sir Arthur Vicars and Pierce O'Mahony.

They left amid stupefied silence. The move cannot have been that unexpected to some of the more senior observers in the room but it certainly upset Shaw. The inquiry had begun at eleven o'clock and, half an hour later, it had lost its star witness and looked to be grinding to a halt. Shaw adjourned proceedings until eleven o'clock the following morning.

Campbell, along with Healy and Vicars (neither of whom had uttered a syllable), went outside to issue their prepared statement. Obviously, they had weighed up the advantages and disadvantages of their chosen course of action. The wording of the warrant had indicated to Campbell that, if Vicars were to agree to co-operate with the commission, all the advantages would lie with the government. Clearly a presumption of guilt already existed; the onus would be on Vicars to prove his innocence.

Then there was the question of whose version of the truth would be more widely accepted. The early press statement by Vicars' champions was an attempt to steal the high ground before the battle. Campbell set out to destroy the credibility of the commission, making it clear to the press and the commissioners that he saw the inquiry as a trap, carefully laid to ensnare Vicars.

However, Vicars had, all along, seen the commission as an invaluable platform. It was a golden opportunity, as he saw it, to exonerate himself from responsibility for the loss of the jewels and to clear his good name. It must have come as a crushing blow when he realised that the commission envisaged by the authorities would not allow him this opportunity.

In the short term at least, the tactics paid off. The press was convinced. The following day's papers poured scorn on the entire shambles. Vicars emerged as the downtrodden and victimised hero of the hour. The commissioners and the government were depicted as the kind of people who would take a shotgun to a butterfly. They had been routed in the first skirmish.

Chester Jones was exasperated. His journey appeared to have been a waste of time. He and his colleagues had been made to look foolish by the adept Campbell. His report to Gladstone would be perfunctory. He told his colleagues that the inquiry was as good as finished. At this stage, nothing useful could be recovered from the wreckage and the commissioners would be advised to hang on to whatever little dignity they had left. He advised Shaw to surrender to the inevitable and abandon proceedings when the commission reconvened.

His colleagues did not argue with him. However, Shaw entered one caveat: the next morning they would announce that they were wrapping up the proceedings but, if the Solicitor General could give any cogent reason for continuing, they would go on.

Day 2 – Saturday 11th January 1908

London

On Saturday morning, the King was breakfasting at Buckingham Palace, though the morning papers were not improving his temper or his appetite. The *Daily Mail* was especially galling. It carried a prominent report on the first day of the Crown Jewels commission. The King learned, for the first time and, much to his chagrin, that the whole inquiry was being conducted in private.

The *Mail* felt that privacy was unfair to Sir Arthur Vicars. Not only that, it suggested disingenuously, but the public would get the impression the government was trying to hide some grave scandal. It then helped the public to come to that conclusion by mentioning that, yes indeed, certain prominent names had already been implicated in current rumours. Another London daily claimed that the government actually knew the identity of the thief and was simply framing Vicars.

The King sent for Knollys. His Secretary was almost as aggravated as he was himself. It had never been the intention of the palace that the inquiry should be conducted in private. Toothless and biased certainly, but not secret. The reaction of the press was as predictable as it was exasperating. Knollys received his instructions from the King: from now on the inquiry was to be conducted in public. Of course, by the time this order was issued, it was already too late to affect that day's proceedings.

Knollys seemed to be under the impression that the concession of publicity would be enough to entice Vicars and his representatives back to the proceedings. He said as much in a message to Gladstone who had, by then, already anticipated Knollys and had issued instructions to Aberdeen, by telegram, that the commission was to abandon its private sessions.

Dublin

Back in Ireland, as they prepared for what they expected to be the second and final day of their inquiry, the commissioners were unaware of the King's reaction.

The scene in the library of the Office of Arms was depressing. It was eleven o'clock. The commissioners were grim. The room was not as crowded as it had been the previous morning as Vicars and his representatives had not had a change of heart overnight. The inquiry looked doomed.

Shaw, almost resignedly, addressed the room. He announced that, owing to the withdrawal of Sir Arthur Vicars and his counsel, neither he, nor his colleagues, saw any point in continuing. Vicars was: '…the only person directly interested in the result of our inquiry, and, without the information which he could give us as the responsible custodian of the jewels which have been lost, any further prosecution of this inquiry could effect no useful purpose and that we should so report to His Excellency. We do not wish, however, to come to any final decision on this matter until we have heard from the Solicitor General the view which the government which he represents takes as to the further proceedings of this commission.'

All eyes turned to the Solicitor General, Redmond Barry. The commissioners were in his hands, almost eager to be despatched by a fatal thumbs down. They had no real desire to preside over the continuation of a commission that looked like it was degenerating into a sorry spectacle.

Then Barry rose and addressed the commission. The government was much more sanguine and felt, he told the surprised commissioners, that the inquiry should go on. His side would produce other witnesses who would be able to throw light on the disappearance of the jewels. This could be done with or without the attendance of Sir Arthur Vicars. The inquiry should continue.

Then Barry added an element of confusion to the sense of futility when he proclaimed that, 'The inquiry is not, as I understand, by any means limited to the mere question of whether or not Sir Arthur Vicars was negligent in his office of custodian.'

This was news to Shaw, and his colleagues, who had spent much of the previous day's abortive half-hour session arguing exactly the opposite with James Campbell. Barry had been sitting a few feet away from him and had made no attempt to contradict him. It was principally on the strength of the limitation of the scope of the inquiry that Campbell had withdrawn.

Shaw made a cursory and obligatory show of independence. He demurred initially and then caved in. Of course, he ventured, the commissioners: '...see, and saw *from the beginning* [my italics]... that it was necessary for us to have before us the whole of the circumstances under which the jewels were abstracted, because it is impossible to say what part of the evidence bearing upon those circumstances may not also bear upon the want of due care and vigilance on the part of Sir Arthur Vicars.'

The government, in the shape of the Solicitor General, was, thereby, given carte blanche to drag whatever element it pleased into the proceedings. Advantage was gleefully taken of such a generous facility. Vicars and his counsel, having already made their flamboyant withdrawal, were not even aware that the ground rules had suddenly changed.

Barry now virtually hijacked the inquiry. He suggested, respectfully of course, that it might be more convenient for him to question the witnesses. The commissioners concurred. They permitted themselves the luxury of asking supplementary questions from time to time, but the thrust of the interrogation was to come from the government's man. Even when it came to supplementary questions, there were to be many occasions when Barry would deflect these by turning (again, respectfully) to the commissioner who had posed the question and telling him that he had been about to ask just such a question and would get around to it presently. Sometimes, if the question was potentially embarrassing to the government, he didn't quite make it.

Without Campbell and Healy present, there was no proper cross-examination. Barry made little attempt to dispel the impression that he was a prosecuting attorney and that Sir Arthur Vicars was the accused. What he presented to the commissioners was little less than a succession of 'prosecution' witnesses. One or two were hostile to the prosecution case but, at no stage, did he attempt to elicit information from any witness that might tend to exonerate Vicars. The commissioners took their cue from him, it was difficult not to.

Barry began his case by drawing the attention of the three men to those Statutes of the Order of St Patrick that related to the safeguarding of the insignia that had, ironically, been compiled by Vicars himself. By reading certain significant statutes, he established that the Crown Jewels should have been 'deposited for safe keeping in a steel safe in the strong-room of the Chancery of the Order in the Office of Arms in Ireland'. Instead of which, he pointed out, they had been lodged in a safe in the library. This point was open to interpretation and could have been challenged had Campbell or Healy been present but, as there was no dissenting voice, the commissioners accepted Barry's contention.

George Dames Burtchaell, Secretary of the Office of Arms, was the first person to be interrogated. He had been a friend and colleague of Vicars since 1893, a fact that showed through on a few occasions as he tried to deflect some of the criticism of Sir Arthur implicit in Barry's questioning. However, his testimony was still an indictment of Vicars' inadequate security precautions. Barry first tackled him on the question of the safe.

'Mr Burtchaell... as we know the present room we are sitting in is the library of the office?'

'Yes.'

'And you see the safe?'

'Yes.'

'Is that the safe in which, to your knowledge, the Insignia of the Grand Master were deposited?'

'Yes.'

'And also some, at least, of the collars and badges of the Knights Companions?'

By now Burtchaell's responses were beginning to have a certain sameness about them. 'Yes,' he replied, for the fourth time.

'But this, of course, we know, is not the strong-room?'

'No.'

'Is there, as a matter of fact, a strong-room in the office?'

'There is.'

It had not taken Barry long to establish that the Crown Jewels were not lodged in what he held to be their proper place. Now he attempted to show that, even during office hours, it was a simple matter to enter the office undetected. Barry pointed towards the front door.

'During the office hours, was that door locked or not?'

'It was not,' Burtchaell was forced to admit.

'The outer door was not locked? Which means, of course,

that anyone coming in there could enter?'

'Yes,' Burtchaell conceded.

'Was there any doorkeeper at all in watch over it?'

Burtchaell grabbed at the proffered straw. 'Oh yes, the messenger.'

'But where did he sit?'

'In his room at the back. The door was opposite, always open, and nobody could come in without his seeing.' Burtchaell was clearly bluffing. He was doing his best for Vicars. He knew that Stivey did not have a clear view of the front door.

Barry called his bluff. 'He had a view right down to the door?' he asked, quizzically.

Burtchaell hedged. 'He would see or hear them.'

Barry next insisted that Burtchaell get up and show him, and the commissioners, the unobstructed view that Stivey had from his room. They all trooped out to have a look. Moments later, they filed back in again. Burtchaell was forced to admit that he had been mistaken. Even if Stivey had been sitting in his room, it would have been possible for someone to enter without his knowledge.

Barry went on to build a solid platform for his case from Burtchaell's testimony. He made much of the fact that the library was used as a waiting room and that persons were often left there alone and unattended. He managed to make it sound as if the theft was all just a simple matter of smashing a glass case, grabbing a handful of gems and dashing out the door. Burtchaell pointed out that he did much of his own work in the library, the essential reading material for his genealogical searches being within easy reach. He even, rather feebly, pointed out that, because the long table in the middle of the room was often covered with books, many visitors might not even see the safe tucked away in the corner of the room.

The crux of Burtchaell's examination came, however, over the question of keys. He was first asked about access to the strong-room. He admitted that he was unsure of the number of keys in existence for this room, it was either three or four. Vicars and Stivey definitely had one each. He had once had a third, which he had returned and which was now in a drawer in the strong-room, and Pierce Gun Mahony had had one. Burtchaell was not sure whether this was a fourth key or whether his key had, at any stage, been given to Mahony.

Barry concentrated on Stivey's key first. The messenger, he was told, had opened the strong-room door in the morning and locked it again at night. During the day, as the door was open whenever Stivey had occasion to leave his own room, he would lock the grille door and leave the key in a drawer in his desk. In a society as hierarchical as that of Edwardian Ireland, it was unusual for someone so junior to be entrusted with so much responsibility. Burtchaell knew this and he did not escape having to admit it.

'Can you,' asked Barry, 'give any information to the commissioners why a messenger should be invested with the keys of the strong-room?'

Burtchaell thought for a moment but was unable to come up with a plausible reason. 'I cannot tell you,' he replied. Barry then went after Mahony's possession of a strong-room key in much the same way. He elicited the fact from Burtchaell that Mahony was a voluntary and part-time functionary.

'Having regard,' he enquired, 'to his position in the office as Cork Herald, an unpaid officer, who came here only on certain occasions, what was the necessity at all, according to your view, of his having a key of the strong-room?'

'Well I do not think there was any necessity. I was not aware that he had a key of the strong-room, I may tell you, until after I heard that the jewels had been lost.'

'And you were not aware of any necessity why he should have had it?'

'No, I do not think so.'

'So that you have told us now that you were really, as I understand, the working official of the office?'

'Yes.'

'And you were able to dispense with the key of the strong-room?'

'I was, because Stivey had one as well as Sir Arthur Vicars.'

Having established that there was no famine of strong-room keys, Barry then went on to demonstrate that there was a veritable feast of front-door keys. Burtchaell told the commission that the mortise lock on the front door was never put on at night. All that was needed to enter the office was a simple latchkey. To the best of his knowledge, there were at least six of these. He had one himself and the rest were in the hands of Vicars, Kerr, Mrs Farrell, Stivey and Mahony. (There was actually a seventh! It belonged to the man responsible for the light in the clock tower during the Castle season.)

Burtchaell was in the witness chair for over an hour. He had tried to duck, deflect and avoid certain questions out of loyalty to Vicars. For example, he allowed the commission to go on thinking, for a while, that both the front-door locks were used. It wasn't until asked a direct question that he admitted only the frail latchkey lay between a would-be thief and the safe containing the Crown Jewels. Despite his protectiveness, he had been an effective 'prosecution' witness. He had hurt Vicars just by telling the truth. Vicars had distributed keys like confetti at a wedding.

Mrs Farrell followed Burtchaell. She was still employed as a cleaner in the Office of Arms, the shake-up had not affected her. She told the commissioners what she had told the police, with one notable omission.

She mentioned that she had found the front door unlocked when she arrived for work on Wednesday 3rd July and that she discovered the strong-room door open on the morning of Saturday 6th July. She even talked about the mysterious visitor of March 1907. This is where she held back.

'Was that gentleman,' Barry asked her, 'any of the officials of the office?'

Her reply was odd. 'That is what I can't make out,' she said. 'I did not know him apparently.'

'Can you identify him now?'

'No, sir.'

Her response had all the hallmarks of police coaching. 'I did not know him *apparently*.' Mrs Farrell had probably been convinced by Kerr and others that, as positive as she had been about having seen Lord Haddo that morning, she just wasn't certain enough to identify him for the inquiry.

William Stivey was down on his luck. Unlike Mrs Farrell, his days at the Office of Arms were over. In the aftermath of the robbery, he had aided and abetted Vicars while significant information had been withheld from the police. When the axe fell, Stivey, having no influential former MPs to plead his case, had no option but to accept his dismissal. He had left the office on 12th October 1907 and, when the call came from the commission to return to his old haunt, he was living among retired military men at the Wesleyan Soldiers Home in Newbridge, County Kildare.

The questioning of Stivey went on for over an hour and a half. In truth, he did little more than confirm what the commissioners had already garnered from Burtchaell. Stivey admitted that he had no real need of a strong-room key. Once the cumbersome metal door was opened in the morning, it was left open. When he was absent for any length of time, he would simply lock the grille door and put the key in his drawer. His absences would include an hour in the middle of the day for dinner and occasional trips to the post office that might keep him away for ten to fifteen minutes. At night, he told the commissioners, the keys of the grille were simply left in the lock and the outer strong-room door was closed over.

Only once had he ever been entrusted with the key of the safe. That was on 6th July 1907.

He was quizzed about the visitors book. He had not been overly conscientious about entering the names of guests. If a group arrived, he would simply write in one name and leave it at that. If the visitor was a regular one, he admitted that he might not include a name at all. Barry was particularly keen to hear about the visits to the office of Mr Esme Percy, a friend of Vicars, and Miss Daisy Newman.

In 1907, Percy was a young actor with Sir Frank Benson's Company, a troupe that made frequent visits to Dublin. He had been in the Office of Arms on more than one occasion although Stivey had only recorded the first visit, with a Mrs Brown Potter, on 12th April 1907. Stivey seemed to think that Percy was, at one stage, staying with Vicars.

Daisy Newman had also come into the office, along with Horlock, sometime in April. She too had returned on her own and had spent some time with Vicars, during which he had given her the 'grand tour'. Vicars had taken down some of the rare books in the library and allowed her to look at them. She had then been shown the strong-room but Stivey was not sure whether or not she had seen the Crown Jewels.

Why, of all people who had visited the office, were these two singled out for special attention? Other names came up in the course of the commission's inquiries, but these are the only names specifically introduced by Barry. At the very least, they were being used by him to illustrate Vicars' irresponsibility and, more than likely, to give an impression that he didn't always mix in the best of circles.

Percy was an actor with a distinguished theatre company. But, even at the beginning of the 20th century, the upper reaches of society still clung to the belief that actors (and, more particularly, actresses) were somehow less than reputable. If Vicars not only knew but housed, Percy, he might be moving in some feckless and dangerously Bohemian circles. Barry was pushing the same button of prejudice when it came to the enigmatic Daisy Newman, offering no explanation as to why he pursued this particular line of enquiry. He left it entirely to the power of suggestion.

Day 3 – Monday 13th January 1908

On Monday morning, the commission reconvened. The fire, once again, burned brightly in the grate. After a day's break, the commissioners were rested. The usual quota of interested Castle officials, such as Police Commissioner Ross and Assistant Commissioner Harrell, took their seats to look on. Outside the Bedford Tower, the reporters continued to cool their heels. Despite the King's explicit instructions, the press was not made welcome. To attend the inquiry, you either had to be an influential official (preferably with a stake in the outcome) or a witness.

At ten thirty, Pierce Gun Mahony seated himself opposite the commissioners to answer Barry's questions, but he was not easily drawn out. His replies were informative and honest, but largely monosyllabic. It was as if he didn't wish to draw too much attention to himself. He might have had a valid reason; he was, after all, the only herald who had survived unscathed. Where he could possibly give a straight 'yes' or 'no', he did just that, only fleshing out his answers when directly requested to do so. He was ill at ease for a man so familiar with the surroundings in which he was giving evidence.

Mahony was quizzed about keys but added little to what the commissioners had already learned from Burtchaell. He had been given a front-door key on occasions when Vicars had been out of the country. In December 1906, Vicars had announced that he was travelling to London and asked Mahony to supervise the office while he was gone. He had handed Mahony a latchkey and a strong-room key. Vicars had never asked for them to be returned. Mahony had only given them back after the theft was discovered on 6th July 1907.

Mahony himself had been absent from the office, through illness, for a lengthy period between April and July 1907. During that time, both keys had been locked in a desk in his house in Burlington Road.

Mahony was well aware that, while Vicars might have had a legitimate reason for giving him keys of the front door and strong-room while he was absent in London, their return should have been sought on his homecoming. Barry was equally well aware of that fact and asked Mahony why he needed to have a strong-room key.

'Well, when I came in here, you see, in the morning I could unlock the strong-room door if anybody else was in and let them get out the books,' he replied.

The Solicitor General wasn't buying that one. 'But Stivey had a key, you know!'

'Yes, but if he had not been in...' he tailed off lamely, '...or anything like that.'

'But it was his habit to be here at ten in the morning.'

'Yes.'

'Your office hours did not begin until eleven.'

'Well mine were absolutely voluntary.'

'For what purpose,' said Barry, ignoring Mahony's tone of injured innocence, 'could the strong-room door require to be opened before eleven in the morning?'

'None that I know of,' admitted Mahony.

'There was no purpose. Then can you suggest why you should have been allowed a key of the strong-room after Sir Arthur Vicars' return, after the Christmas of 1906?'

'I cannot make any suggestion.'

After an hour, Mahony was allowed to step down. He was followed by two more key holders, John O'Keefe, the Board of Works official responsible for the light in the Bedford Tower clock during the Castle season and who professed not to have known of the existence of the Crown Jewels before their disappearance, and Detective Owen Kerr, who made the same admission. Following the confession of the detective's strange lack of awareness, the commissioners adjourned for lunch.

On the resumption, Horlock made his mark for the first and only time. Vicars' loyal Private Secretary resolutely refused to give evidence. Beard had been sent upstairs to find him. While the commissioners and Barry patiently awaited his arrival, Horlock was telling the Secretary to the Commission that he respectfully declined to attend. He objected to the affair being conducted in private and he felt that his former chief was not getting fair play.

Francis Bennett Goldney was apprehensive about the summons from the inquiry. He knew he could ignore it but he worried about the construction that would be put on his absence if he did. He had been badly shaken by the events of the last few months.

Things had been going well for him. As Mayor of Canterbury, the local blue-blooded 'county' types who ran the Conservative Party had been forced to take him seriously. What they didn't have to do was like him – and they didn't. In fact, the local grandees feared and detested him as he represented something new. He was capable, clever, palpably ambitious and determined to make a career in politics. A little becoming detachment might have served him better, he was just a shade too eager for advancement for aristocratic Tory tastes.

But the Crown Jewels controversy had put him in an awkward situation. He was about to present himself as the next Conservative

Party candidate for Canterbury (the sitting MP wanted to retire). The Crown Jewels affair could become a major embarrassment, possibly an insurmountable obstacle. To protect this vulnerable flank, he had started to distance himself from Vicars some time previously. The two men had spent a month together in Abbot's Barton in September 1907 where they had fuelled each other's belief in Shackleton's guilt and then had laid siege to Scotland Yard with their theories. On his return to Ireland, Vicars had invited Goldney to join him in Dublin. Goldney, however, had declined.

Goldney's reaction to the summons from the inquiry was one of alarm. Being relatively isolated, he might not have been aware of just how powerless the commission was. He had few newspaper reports to rely on and he was unable to talk to those who had already been examined. He feared that the inquiry might have been given a very wide-ranging brief. There were certain things about the Office of Arms that he did not want to discuss. The slightest breath of scandal would have been enough to end his embryonic political career. However, he couldn't very well refuse to give evidence, nor could he refuse to answer any questions that he might be asked. Neither option would have been politically prudent.

When he visited Dublin, it was Goldney's habit to stay at St James' Terrace with Vicars. But when he travelled over on Sunday 12th January 1908, he went straight to the Shelbourne Hotel to check in. He justified this move on the basis that the commission would not take too kindly to him staying in the house of the subject of their investigation. He had a point, but that was not the real reason for his unwillingness to follow his old ritual. The sooner people forgot all about his friendship with Sir Arthur

Vicars and his association with the Office of Arms, the happier he would be.

His first session with Barry and the commissioners produced nothing sensational or even very interesting. He was not as reluctant as those who had gone before him to say anything that would reflect badly on Vicars. He was quite prepared to damn his friend both with faint praise and polite criticism.

He had seen the jewels twice, he told the commissioners. On both occasions, there had been others present. The first time he had seen them was on one of Vicars' informal tours around the time of the opening of the International Exhibition in May 1907. While Vicars was proudly displaying the jewels, Goldney had noticed a 'stranger' entering the library. Vicars was deep in conversation with Lady Orford, one of the group, and paid no attention to the newcomer. Lady Orford was declaring what a great pity it was to have such fine gems locked away. Goldney watched the stranger, he was listening intently.

'It occurred to me,' he ventured to the commissioners, 'that it was an imprudent thing – I would not say perhaps that it was imprudent – but that it was a curious thing to have such a conversation in a stranger's presence.'

He was to find out later that the man hadn't been a stranger at all. Goldney had subsequently been introduced to him but he could not supply the commission with the man's name. However, on this flimsy pretext, he had been able to hint to the inquiry that all was not as it should have been in the Office of Arms. Although disowning his own use of the word 'imprudent', he managed nonetheless to get it on the record twice.

His main contribution in his first spell in the witness box

came almost as an afterthought. He had not added much to the sum of anyone's knowledge and, in virtual desperation, Barry simply asked him straight out if he had anything of importance to tell the inquiry. Goldney suddenly became coy. 'Well sir,' he said, 'I am in this difficulty, that I do not know how much to say, or how little, or how far I would be justified in stating things that might only tend to raise suspicions.'

'I am not asking you to state your suspicions,' replied Barry.

'No,' agreed Goldney, 'in fact, I do not suspect anybody as being guilty of taking the jewels. Whether, in my mind, I suspect that certain persons may know something about it, is another matter.'

Suddenly Goldney became interesting. He went on to say that he would be obliged to answer any questions at a sworn inquiry. But that here, he could not be put on oath and was reluctant to introduce anything which might prove to be unfounded or irrelevant. The Chairman ordered the shorthand writer to stop taking notes. Goldney spoke freely.

When he had finished, Shaw, for the record, indicated to Goldney that what he had said had no bearing on the inquiry. It was a curious episode and it was to have a sequel. On Tuesday, Goldney would return to the stand and repeat virtually everything he had already said off the record. Except on that day his evidence was recorded and the commission, by pursuing this particular line, judged it to be relevant to their inquiry, after all.

The final witness on the third day was Assistant Police Commissioner Harrel. He managed, finally, to exonerate Phillips, the unfortunate coachman who had been named as a suspect by Vicars. The police had established his innocence to their satisfaction and Vicars had made some amends by paying his passage to America.

Harrel was also tackled on the subject of the mysterious Daisy Newman. He was asked did he know anything about her and replied ambiguously, 'Yes, I know everything about her.' He did not expand on this cryptic comment but certainly managed to reinforce Barry's attempt to convey the impression that the Office of Arms had regularly played host to some dubious characters.

Day 4 – Tuesday 14th January 1908

At ten thirty on Tuesday morning Francis Bennett Goldney 'presented himself again' to the commissioners. He had more to get off his chest. He wished to be allowed to add one or two things to what he had already said and the commission was quite happy to hear him. They hadn't exactly got very much out of him the previous day other than some mischievous commentary. Goldney, it appeared, was anxious to present some telegrams to the commission. They were from Vicars and were mostly dated October 1907.

Sir Arthur, it transpired, had entered into an unwise financial arrangement from which Goldney was trying to extricate him. In his efforts to help, Goldney had signed a bill on Vicars' behalf. For a judge, Shaw's cross-examination seems strangely inept. He dived in feet first.

'That was not the bill to which you referred yesterday?' he asked.

'Yesterday?' replied Goldney, archly.

'In which Mr Shackleton was [involved]?' responded Shaw, without standing down the note-taker.

'Yes. The bill which I had signed.'

What Shaw had done was to ensure that the inadmissible information that Goldney had conveyed the previous day, and that he had been obviously eager to impart for his own reasons, was now on the record. What was considered irrelevant and struck out on Monday was suddenly deemed pertinent on Tuesday. Goldney was then allowed to detail, at great length, the peculiar financial arrangements that had been entered into, at various times, by Shackleton, Vicars and himself. It is apparent that these dealings had a lot to do with the bad blood that now existed between the three men.

Goldney's story is complex. In 1906 Vicars had signed a bill for £600 for Shackleton. This was a form of guarantee, it did not mean that Vicars had lent Shackleton money. The actual money had been advanced by a third party but only on the strength of Vicars' signature on a 'bill'. Effectively, he was guarantor for the return, with interest, of the £600 and, if Shackleton defaulted, Vicars would be liable to pay back the money. Goldney had also become Shackleton's guarantor for a larger sum at the same time.

In the spring of 1907, Shackleton had visited Goldney at Abbot's Barton in a flap. It was a Saturday and he needed a hefty sum, £1,500, by Monday. He gave Goldney the impression that the money was not for him but for Vicars. Furthermore, he added, Goldney needn't worry about a thing, the money would be paid back before the end of the week. Goldney was uncomfortable. He did not entirely trust Shackleton but, as he understood the money was for Vicars he agreed, reluctantly, to sign the bill. Shackleton was relieved and grateful. He thanked Goldney and told him that his family's solicitor would be down that evening and he would have all the relevant material for Goldney to sign.

As Goldney waited, his temper grew short. He began to feel somewhat used. He started to wonder whether these demands on his money would become even greater once he became established in the Office of Arms. Finally, the solicitor arrived. The man did not conform to Goldney's view of the polite and self-effacing family solicitor.

'I suppose you know what business I've come on?' he opened. Goldney replied that he did.

'You are Mayor of Canterbury?'

Goldney was not interested in trading small talk. 'You must find that out from other people,' he retorted.

The stranger sensed a certain chill and decided to get on with his business. 'Are you prepared to sign this bill?' he asked.

'I do not like it but, as it is to please Sir Arthur Vicars, I will do it.'

Much later, Goldney discovered the truth about the 'solicitor'. He was a well-known moneylender. Goldney had not done anything to assist Vicars, who was unaware of the whole transaction, he had simply got Shackleton out of a hole. What's more, the money was not paid back by the end of the week.

In October 1907, Goldney had passed on all the documentation relevant to the transaction to his solicitor, who had begun to exert pressure on Shackleton and his family. The money was paid and the bills cancelled. This was done, according to Goldney, not by Shackleton himself, but by his brother Ernest, the polar explorer. Ernest Shackleton had, according to his biographer Roland Huntford, borrowed £1,000 to help repay his brother's loans partly to save him from insolvency and partly because: 'Had

Frank Shackleton gone bankrupt, it would have destroyed what remained of Ernest Shackleton's credit.'

During Goldney's discourse, Barry was strangely silent. All the questions, for once, were coming from the three commissioners. The reason for his standoffishness became clear when Goldney addressed him directly. 'Please understand this,' Goldney said, 'I do not want to prejudice you against any member of the office.'

Barry was no fool. He knew very well that was exactly Goldney's intention. He was also aware that this was an unsworn inquiry and that no statement made was subject to privilege of any kind. If anyone felt defamed or slandered by anything said at the inquiry, they had every right to take legal action. Barry was not going to step onto this enticing expanse of quicksand.

When, out of the blue, Goldney tossed this disingenuous remark at him, Barry turned quickly to the note-taker. 'Mr Goldney addressing me, says that he does not want to prejudice me against anyone. But it is not for me; it is for the commissioners to find out all about this matter. What comes before you here is a voluntary statement by Mr Goldney.' With that he passed the buck, neatly, back to the commissioners. They juggled with it, clumsily, for a few seconds and then, desperately threw it to Goldney. His statement, reiterated the three commissioners, had been voluntary and unsolicited.

Goldney spent about forty minutes on the stand, far longer than on the previous day. He had done little to clarify anything, but he had succeeded in bringing the wisdom of the commissioners into doubt. In effect, he had bamboozled them. He had behaved much like a clever attorney who asks a question he knows will be disallowed, in order to convey evidence he knows is inadmissible but that will help his client.

If any villain was to emerge from the commission, Goldney would make sure it was not going to be him. Instead, he was intent on giving the commissioners some ammunition that they could employ against Shackleton. He was using Shackleton to draw their fire.

Day 5 – Wednesday 15th January 1908

The fifth day of evidence was spent examining police witnesses in the particulars of the case. When Commissioner Sir John Ross was questioned, no suggestion was made that perhaps his officers, or even he himself, might have made greater efforts to protect the Crown Jewels. There was no minute and searching examination of the security around Dublin Castle. Nobody even hinted that the police could have been more vigilant.

The most authoritative and informative evidence that day came, as one might expect, from Inspector John Kane, who had made his way across from Scotland Yard. Having nothing to lose, he was easily the most forthcoming of all the police witnesses. He was questioned, for example, about the mysterious piece of ribbon detached from the Badge. He was asked had he any theory about it and duly supplied one.

'We will assume,' he said, 'that some person conversant with the place… would have time to remove it and would remove it at his leisure. It would be useless to an ordinary thief or house-breaker, or burglar coming in, to take that trouble. To me it is incomprehensible that any ordinary burglar should do so.'

Jones intervened. 'Something that would lead to identification if he forgot it after he had disposed of the jewels?' he asked.

Kane was non-committal, 'There are so many explanations to give of that ribbon.'

Barry then offered one such explanation. 'Might it not happen,' he asked, 'that it might have been left in the hope that at some time the jewels might have been restored by a person who took them for a temporary purpose?'

'Well,' replied Kane, 'that suggestion will hardly apply to an outside thief.'

It is through Kane's testimony that something of substance emerges from the inquiry. He repeatedly ventured the opinion that the theft was an 'inside' job, in whole or in part. He told the commission that Vicars had disagreed with him but had subsequently changed his mind on the subject.

At first, Kane was reluctant to mention Shackleton by name. Barry, however, knew who he was talking about. He indicated to the witness and the commission that, as the person had already been mentioned by name before the commission, there would be no harm in Kane doing so as well. Kane related that, on 28th August, in a conversation with Kane, Vicars had implicated Shackleton.

Kane had pointed out to Vicars that Shackleton had been out of the country when the jewels were stolen. 'I put that to him several times,' Kane said, 'and then he suggested that Shackleton was in collusion with other persons in this robbery.'

'Were those other persons in the office?' Barry asked.

'No,' replied Kane. 'They were not in the office at all, and never were, as far as I could ascertain.'

We know from the Bulmer Hobson article that Vicars had

implicated Richard Howard Gorges as well as Shackleton. From Kane's answer, it is plain that he had taken the accusation seriously enough to examine the background of Gorges. Kane had intimated earlier that he did not believe that the robbery had taken place on the night of 5th July. He was queried about this. Did he not think, when he was investigating the theft, that the robbery of the jewels and the opening of the strong-room had taken place on the same night?

'No, I did not,' was his reply.

'Do you believe,' asked Starkie, 'that the opening of the strong-room door was to account for the disappearance of the jewels?'

'I believe that... the strong-room door was purposely opened that night for the purpose of bringing about an investigation that would lead to the discovery of a robbery that had taken place before Friday night, the 5th of July.'

Kane felt the same about the discovery of the unlocked front door on Wednesday 3rd July as well. It was ironic that neither attempt to highlight the theft had actually expedited its discovery. 'We know,' said Kane, 'that the persons who found those doors open did not do what one would have expected they would have done, rush off to the police at once and report it.'

Jones understood his logic. 'The leaving open of the front door,' he ventured, 'not being sufficient in the first instance they used stronger measures?'

Kane agreed. 'If I may use the phrase,' he said, 'they thought they would go one better this time.' Later, he added that he felt the safe was left unlocked on the Friday night as well, even though the jewels had been taken some time before that.

Kane was then asked why the person or persons who had

opened the front door and the strong-room door, had wanted to precipitate an investigation. His reply was guarded and enigmatic.

'There was,' he said, 'a certain high personage coming here, and possibly certain people thought that when these jewels had disappeared it would be necessary that some explanation of that should be forthcoming before their arrival.'

Kane refused to be drawn further on the subject. He said that he was not there under the protection of his superiors and that he really only had a right to state facts, not express opinions.

Kane's testimony is invaluable and intriguing. In brief, reading between the lines, his theory was that some member of the Office of Arms had got hold of Vicars' keys. That person had then used exact copies, or the originals, to steal the jewels sometime before the 3rd July. The jewels had been taken temporarily, possibly with the intention of raising money on them quickly, redeeming them within days and replacing them. Either that or they were stolen for a ransom of some kind. Something had then gone badly wrong. Perhaps it had not been possible to redeem the jewels. It was then essential to provide an alibi for the person who had stolen them. The King was due in Ireland and as the unidentified member of the Office of Arms was expected to be in the country prior to his arrival, the theft had to be discovered quickly or the 'inside man' would fall under suspicion. A co-conspirator had left indicators that should have been sufficient to hasten the discovery of the theft, but they had been ignored. Had it not been for the return of Lord de Ros' collar, the fact of the robbery would not have emerged until well into the royal visit, when Vicars would have had occasion to take the jewels out of the safe for use by Aberdeen.

If that is a correct reading of Kane's mind, it eliminates all but two suspects for the 'inside' role: Francis Bennett Goldney and Francis Shackleton, both of whom were out of the country in late June and early July but who were both due to be in Dublin for the King's visit.

Day 6 – Thursday 16th January 1908

The inquiry was running out of steam. In the continuing absence of Vicars, there was almost no one left to examine. Only one major witness – Frank Shackleton – had not been questioned by the commissioners. He was in San Remo, Italy, when he read that the inquiry was to take place and had wired Sir James Dougherty asking whether he would be needed to give evidence. On Monday 13th, the letter asking him to appear was forwarded from his club in London. He left as soon as he got the summons and travelled for three days, arriving in Dublin early on the morning of Thursday 16th January.

He was visibly tired as he sat down in the witness chair. He was also somewhat nervous. He wasn't quite sure what had been said already but he had got a nasty shock sitting through the preceding testimony in which a DMP investigating officer had been asked about the suspicions of Vicars and had named Shackleton as Vicars' prime suspect.

This was not exactly news to Shackleton, but having it aired publicly indicated the trend the inquiry was taking. He was relieved that there were no reporters in the room. He had also been tipped off about the 'facts' that Goldney had presented to the commission concerning the financial dealings in the Office of

Arms and must have known that he would face some searching questions about his own involvement in those transactions.

In the library of the Office of Arms, waiting for Shackleton's evidence, were Police Commissioner Ross and Assistant Under Secretary Dougherty, among others. As Shackleton made himself comfortable in the witness chair, Barry spoke. He suggested that, as he had no idea what Shackleton might have to add to the sum of their knowledge, he would leave it to the commissioners to examine him. Barry had a well-developed, self-protective sense – if he didn't already know the answers, he preferred to let someone else ask the questions.

Chairman Shaw made most of the running. He took Shackleton through his introduction to the Office of Arms before getting to the main point of his examination, the Dublin Herald's relationship with Vicars. Shackleton told him that he shared a house with Vicars and paid half the rent and expenses. Shaw then began to ask him about the bills that Vicars had signed for him. Shackleton got as far as telling him that there had been two, one for £650, when he stopped. He had spotted the note-taker and began to put two and two together.

'None of this will appear in the press?' he asked, anxiously.

'This will be taken down,' replied Shaw.

That was already obvious to Shackleton, but he remained polite and measured. 'I do not mind a bit, so long as it does not appear in the press. It would be very unpleasant to me if these things came out.'

'I must warn you before you go any further,' admonished Shaw, 'that what you are saying now is being taken down by a shorthand writer; it will be printed and it may be published.'

Shackleton's politeness evaporated.

'Then I consider,' he retorted indignantly, 'that I should have been told of this beforehand.' He paused to calm himself. 'I do not mean it disrespectfully but I think it is rather unfair that I should have been allowed to make these statements, because it is a serious matter in business.'

'But you were told that you need not answer.'

'I was given to understand that the investigation was private. It has been stated in the papers that it is private.'

'It is private in this sense,' replied Shaw, 'that the public are not present here; but the evidence is being taken down and will be printed and may be published.'

'Then I think that the statement should have been given to me before. My reason is this, that it would be very injurious to me in business were it known that at a period when I was engaged in a rather large business transaction I was absolutely in monetary difficulties to any extent.'

Having made his protest, Shackleton then took up his explanation where he had left off. He decided that the damage, if any, had already been done.

The explanation of his financial dealings with Vicars and Goldney was detailed and tedious but its conclusion was an extraordinary one. To back up certain claims he was making, he handed the commissioners the letter he had received from Vicars, postmarked 'Abbot's Barton, Canterbury' and dated the 25th August 1907. It dealt mainly with financial arrangements between the three former friends but he drew the attention of the commissioners to the conclusion (already quoted), a complete non sequitur claiming that Shackleton knew the whereabouts of the jewels and expressing the hope that he would tell Kane 'everything calculated to facilitate matters'.

The commissioners could not ignore Vicars' (familiar) allegation. One assumes they were not meant to. Shackleton knew that, sooner or later, he would be questioned on Sir Arthur's suspicions. So he introduced the subject himself and in a context that was to his best advantage. Shaw questioned him on the reference and Shackleton was prepared for battle. He positively seethed with righteous indignation as he accounted for the allegation. While staying in Harrogate, he had been shown a newspaper report that the jewels had been found. He had then dashed off letters to Mahony and Vicars asking why he had not been told about it.

Mahony had replied that there was no truth in the report, the jewels had not been found. Before he received Mahony's reply, Shackleton had met Goldney at his club.

'Why didn't you tell me the jewels were recovered?' Shackleton had asked.

'Are they?' had been Goldney's reply.

'Yes.'

'I never heard of it. Are you sure?'

'Yes,' replied Shackleton. 'I heard it on good authority.'

Shackleton didn't explain to the commissioners why he had not told Goldney the actual source of his information (a newspaper report) and none of them saw fit to ask. On the strength of the letter to Vicars and the conversation in the club, Goldney had gone to Scotland Yard and told Kane that Shackleton knew where the jewels were hidden. It was a ludicrous and patently unsupportable allegation. Shackleton felt totally safe in handing over Vicars' letter to the commissioners. He was engaging them on ground of his own choosing. The commissioners, in effect at his behest, had begun their questioning about the suspicions of Vicars in a way that totally discredited those suspicions. It was a neat stroke.

Shackleton then had some more of Vicars' charges thrown at him. There was Sir Arthur's theory that he had returned to Ireland from 28th to 30th June, stayed in a Dublin hotel, taken Vicars' front-door key and stolen the jewels. Shackleton denied having done this. He told the commissioners that the police had accounted for most of his movements in the few days preceding the theft.

As the interrogation continued, Shackleton became more and more confident. He began to drop important names. He made no secret of his friendship with Lord Ronald Sutherland Gower and his association with the King's brother-in-law, the Duke of Argyll. At various times, he nonchalantly called on eminent public servants like Sir John Ross and Sir James Dougherty to help him remember dates or verify facts. He adopted a posture of disarming frankness when he was asked about his access to Vicars' keys. He candidly admitted that, although he didn't have a front-door key of the tower, he could easily have had wax impressions made of any of Vicars' keys. He stated, quite baldly, that he could have taken the safe key while Vicars was taking a bath or was otherwise occupied.

These admissions helped his credibility and did nothing at all to assist Vicars' case. Shaw suggested as much. 'And the keys were there for you to take possession in the way you say?' he asked.

'I could easily have taken possession of them,' Shackleton asserted.

'During the time he was in his bath?'

'I could have taken it [the safe key] and kept it for a week and put a key almost like it on the chain, trusting to his never having occasion to go to the safe for another week or so. Anyone could have done that. I don't want to pile up a case against myself, but it would be quite easy for me to do so.'

His judicious honesty meant he was virtually exonerating himself and in the process piling up the case against Vicars. He alluded to his doubts about the security of the office, those same *post facto* doubts that had so annoyed Vicars back in July. He managed to slip in, in passing, reminders that Vicars had not investigated the open strong-room on the Saturday morning and that, while Vicars trusted Stivey, a mere messenger, with the safe key, he, a Herald, had never had it in his possession.

Barry had taken a back seat during most of the questioning, allowing the commissioners, mainly Shaw, to make most of the running. He had asked a few supplementary questions to satisfy his own curiosity, but had left it at that. After Shackleton had been in the chair for about an hour and a half, he intervened. There was something he wanted to get on the record. 'You say that suspicion has been thrown on you,' he observed. 'I must ask you a definite question, and you will understand that you need not answer it if you do not like. Did you, or did you not take the jewels?'

Barry got the answer one might expect from a man who had steadfastly denied committing the crime and who wasn't even under oath. 'I did not take them,' said Shackleton. 'I know nothing of their disappearance; I have no suspicion of anybody.'

'Were you concerned, directly or indirectly, in their taking?'

'No.'

'Did anyone in confederacy with you take the jewels?'

'No. I had no hand in it, nor do I know anybody that took them, nor have I the least suspicion.'

'Or have you any idea as to where they are?'

'No, not the least idea as to where they are.'

'Have you heard any speculation from anyone as to where the jewels may be?'

'No, sir, other than I was told they were back in the office. I know perfectly well that I am accused of even aiding Lord Haddo in taking them away.'

The allusion caused consternation. That had clearly been Shackleton's intention.

'You need not mention that,' Barry said sharply.

'I am only mentioning what has been said.'

The rest of Shackleton's questioning was desultory and he stepped down shortly afterwards. His examination had lasted for nearly two hours, far longer than anyone else's. He had been subjected to detailed scrutiny and he had handled himself with an aplomb that impressed the commissioners.

He had certainly won over Barry, who then asked that Inspector Kane be recalled, he wanted to clear up a few points regarding Shackleton. The inspector was asked about the suspicions of Vicars and Goldney. He restated that they had approached him on many occasions with charges against Shackleton.

'But,' he said, 'they never could give me any tangible evidence that satisfied me that there was any justification for those suggestions at all.'

Shaw asked, 'Did they show you any letter on which they founded their suggestions?'

'No,' Kane replied, 'they did not. It was merely on conversations that came to their knowledge which Mr Shackleton had had with other people.'

'Did you ever trace any fact that would tend to throw suspicion on Mr Shackleton?' asked Starkie.

'Never.'

'Not a shred of evidence against him?'

'Not the remotest. I have repeated to Sir Arthur Vicars and his friends over and over again, and I desire to say that now, when they pestered me, not only with suggestions but with direct accusations of Mr Shackleton, that they might as well accuse me, so far as the evidence they produced went to justify them.'

The commission now dribbled to a conclusion. Miss Gibbon, the typist, was called, to see what she knew. Like Horlock before her, and for the same avowed reason, Miss Gibbon refused to co-operate with the inquiry. Shortly after that the commission adjourned.

It had sat for six days in all. The commissioners had interviewed twenty-two people at least once. Six witnesses had been questioned twice and two had been examined three times. Three more had refused to co-operate entirely. The commissioners had heard over 120,000 words of explanation, admission, justification and accusation. The inquiry had begun by being thrown into confusion and had then changed its colours, like a chameleon, by alternately narrowing and then widening its scope.

It had had to rely on the willingness of witnesses to appear and to answer any questions put to them. It could not entirely trust the answers given because they were not given under oath. It could not force witnesses to hand over relevant documents unless they chose to do so. It appeared to invert the normal legal process by presuming the guilt of Sir Arthur Vicars until he was able to satisfy the inquiry of his innocence. He chose not to attempt to do so. In the end, it is difficult to see what purpose it all served.

Perhaps, as his own evidence concluded, Shackleton had wondered at the impressive array of power and prestige that had turned up to listen to his testimony. Ross, Dougherty and Harrel had dropped in from time to time to hear the testimony of other witnesses. The two policemen had given evidence, Harrel did so three times. But, over the six days, the three men had not often been in the library together, all had better things to do.

However, on that Thursday morning, 16th January, they had dropped in to the Office of Arms for a reason. They wanted to listen to Shackleton's statement, but that wasn't all. They had other business with Shackleton. When the inquiry adjourned, the commissioners left to begin considering the evidence and compile their report.

Shackleton made to leave the Office of Arms for the last time. If he was feeling in any way nostalgic, he had little time to indulge the emotion. As he walked into the corridor outside the library, he was stopped by Harrel who asked him to join himself, Ross and Dougherty in the state offices. Shackleton agreed. Closeted with Harrel and the other two officials, he was presented with evidence of his homosexual activities. He was told that no charges were being pressed but that he was now *persona non grata* in

Dublin. As the New York *Gaelic American* put it in an exultant article: 'Mr Shackleton's whole private life was turned inside out – evidence of his disgusting misconduct was dragged to light, and after having been cross-examined by the detectives at great length he was let go with the admonition to leave the country as quickly as possible.'

Shackleton left Ireland that day. He had no particular reason to return and there is no evidence that he ever did so.

8

Vicars Bows Out

'*Sodom and Gomorrah were destroyed by fire, but Dublin Castle still stands.*'

New York *Gaelic American*, 4th July 1908

THE ATTITUDE OF the journalistic profession towards the Viceregal Commission of Inquiry into the Crown Jewels was coloured by the fact of the proceedings having taken place in camera without good reason. Journalists rarely give the benefit of the doubt to somebody who appears to have something to hide and usually give that person a 'bad press'. In addition, until the inquiry concluded, Sir Arthur Vicars was the only person talking publicly because he was the only one in a position to do so. What the press was printing was, by and large, his gloss on events.

On Tuesday 14th January 1908, for example, the *Daily Express* correspondent spoke to O'Mahony, who made no direct accusations, but intimated that there were rumours around Dublin connecting the name of 'a certain person' with the crime. He observed, enigmatically, that 'some curious circumstances would have been brought to light if Sir Arthur Vicars was able to give evidence at a public and judicial inquiry'.

Most papers sympathised with Vicars. The *Daily Mail*, on 17th January, accused the government of defaming Vicars by spreading lies about him and condemned the handling of the affair as a 'muddle which has rarely been surpassed even in the dismal story of Irish maladministration, and the only remedy for it is a fresh inquiry held in public, since the secret investigation has now virtually reached its conclusion'. The *Mail* also attacked Sir Anthony MacDonnell (something for which this Conservative journal had a particular penchant) saying that he was responsible for every last detail of the commission's procedures.

The renewed interest in the case brought on by the inquiry led some papers to come up with so-called investigative 'scoops'. On 15th January, the London *Tribune* announced that the jewels were still intact and that the object of the theft was to obtain a ransom. The paper went on to claim that one of the perpetrators of the crime was still at large while another was in jail, though no evidence was advanced to support these claims. The *Globe* alleged that the government, in the form of Sir James Dougherty, and the police, in the shape of Sir John Ross, had colluded with the commissioners in order to secure a desirable outcome.

It is clear from newspaper reports that Vicars was winning the propaganda battle hands down, illustrating the benefits of being free to speak while your opponent is muzzled. Behind the scenes, however, he was losing the war badly.

The commission did not take long to reach its verdict. It con-

firmed what MacDonnell had held to be the case all along:
Vicars had been careless. On 26th January, five days before its
official publication, a copy of the final report had been sent to
Aberdeen, the man who had appointed the commissioners. The
verdict saddened rather than surprised him, but it pleased
MacDonnell immensely. His stand had been vindicated and
there would be no holding back any longer. Confirmation had
come from an independent source that Vicars did not deserve to
hold on to his job.

Vicars got the bad news a day in advance of the publication of
the report. It wasn't even an ultimatum: it was simply notification
of a *fait accompli*. The letter, sent on 30th January, informed Vicars
that: 'Letters Patent had passed the Great Seal of Ireland revoking
the Letters Patent that had made him Ulster King of Arms in
1893.' In plain English, it meant that he was no longer being
offered the option of resigning, he was being fired. Vicars was
given a day to hand over the keys of the office and any other
crown property in his custody, to his successor, Neville Rodwell
Wilkinson, who had been appointed with startling rapidity.
Vicars had a day to clear out his own paraphernalia and expunge
all traces of his existence from the Office of Arms. He had occupied the post of Ulster King of Arms for over fourteen years and
disputed his dismissal with the government for three months.
Now that they had an excuse to be rid of him, the Castle authorities did so promptly and ruthlessly.

The report itself summarised the evidence that the three commissioners had heard. First Vicars was criticised for distributing
keys of the office and strong-room with more regard for conven-
ience than security. It was observed that he was foolish to carry

a key to the safe about with him. The safe was only rarely opened, officially at least, and it should have been possible to deposit the key with his banker. Of course to have taken such a practical precaution would have deprived Vicars of one of the pleasures of his life, showing off the jewels to visitors.

There was one unusual feature of the report – Shackleton got a paragraph all to himself. The commissioners referred to the rumours of his complicity, which still abounded:

> *We think it only due to that gentleman to say that he came from San Remo at great inconvenience to give evidence before us, that he appeared to us to be a perfectly truthful and candid witness, and that there was no evidence whatever before us to support the suggestion that he was the person who stole the jewels.*

The report also dealt with the days prior to the theft and the loss of the jewels. It condemned Vicars out of hand for ignoring the warning signs and the news passed on to him by Mrs Farrell via Stivey. The concluding section was reserved for the final judgement on Vicars. The commissioners observed that 'we feel bound to report to Your Excellency that, in our opinion, Sir Arthur Vicars did not exercise due vigilance or proper care as the custodian of the Regalia'.

Suddenly opinion changed. Papers like the *Globe*, which two weeks before had accused Judge Shaw of conspiring with Dougherty to subvert the inquiry, now admitted that 'unless the commissioners are hopelessly at sea in their findings he must be credited with a very serious failure to exercise proper vigilance'.

The *Standard* opined that 'the removal of the responsible custodian of the jewels should satisfy the public that its interests have been properly protected'.

On 31st January 1908, the same day as the commission's report was appearing in the newspapers, the unionist *Irish Times* carried a letter from Vicars in which he outlined the history of the attempts to dismiss him. *The Irish Times*, no lover of the Liberal administration in Ireland, offered some editorial sympathy. The paper claimed to hold no brief for Vicars but criticised the privacy and scope of the commission and insisted that no report emanating from such a commission would satisfy anyone. It demanded a free and open investigation and went on to mention the gossip and scandalous stories that were doing the rounds as well as the accusations against the Irish government that 'it was more anxious to hush up the loss of the jewels than to secure their recovery'. The paper concluded by trumpeting the accusation that 'the Irish government cannot afford... to answer, these grave statements'.

Another paper that had revelled in the embarrassment of the Irish executive was the *Pall Mall Gazette*, a British Conservative daily with a devotion to attacking the jugular of the Liberal administration. It consistently portrayed Vicars as a lonely Tory fighting an unequal battle against Liberal ogres, such as the unspeakable Augustine Birrell. During the controversy over the inquiry, the paper said of Birrell that, while others who had held the post were hated by certain sections of the community in Ireland: 'Mr Birrell is merely despised by all sections, and that with an absolute unanimity which entitles him, if so disposed, to boast that he is the first man in history who has ever realised the ideal of a really united Ireland.'

The *Gazette* showed its true colours in an editorial that attacked the role of MacDonnell and Ross in the affair mentioning a significant connection between the two men, namely that both were Roman Catholics. Not only was the paper determined to turn the Crown Jewels case into an anti-Liberal crusade, it was prepared to imply that the sacking of Vicars constituted a Roman Catholic attack on the Protestant Ascendancy. The notion never took root because, although there were obvious political considerations in the sacking of Vicars, they had little to do with his political beliefs. Although of a unionist stripe, these were seldom articulated. An Irish government, led by Conservatives, would probably have treated Vicars in much the same way.

The *Pall Mall Gazette*'s interest in the controversy tailed off after the publication of the commission's report. So did that of every other British and most Irish newspapers. A fresh sensation had taken over the headlines: King Carlos of Portugal and his son, the Crown Prince, had been assassinated in Lisbon. Vicars and the Crown Jewels commission were suddenly yesterday's news.

On the same day that the papers carried the inquiry findings, most reported, briefly, that Captain Neville Rodwell Wilkinson had become Ulster King of Arms 'in the room of Sir Arthur Vicars'. Wilkinson was not the first choice to replace Vicars. The job had been offered to two others while the controversy over his dismissal had raged. Wisely, both men had decided not to become embroiled in the affair. But Wilkinson was the type who tended to leap in where wise men should fear to tread. In his memoirs, he makes no reference at all to the story that was current at the time of his appointment, relating to the manner in which he came by his job.

Wilkinson was the son-in-law of the Earl of Pembroke, who was a member of the British Privy Council. At a council meeting, the proposed dismissal of Vicars came up and opinions were canvassed about a successor. Pembroke mentioned his son-in-law: he was something of an artist, the painting of crests being one of his hobbies. Though, Pembroke warned that, as far as he was aware, he knew nothing about genealogy and little about heraldry either. The King dismissed this caveat. 'Is he honest?' he asked.

'Yes,' said the Earl.

'Then he'll do,' replied the King.

Wilkinson's appointment was effected with great speed and deftness. Haste was essential because the Viceregal Court was about to move into Dublin Castle for the season and a new Ulster King of Arms was needed to officiate at the various functions that would take place. The swiftness of the appointment of Wilkinson did not go unnoticed. One Dublin newspaper observed that the rapidity of the move would be welcome in other, more important, areas of decision making.

Wilkinson didn't have to wait long for his first crisis. Vicars had been instructed to hand over his keys before midday on Saturday 1st February 1908. The office was to be closed on 31st January to allow him to return what was not his and take away whatever was. Vicars had no intention of going back to the office himself. He sent a clerk instead, presumably from his solicitor Meredith's office. The emissary was refused admission. Vicars now had a ready excuse for a little mischief of his own. What he did reflected his bitterness – he refused to hand over his keys.

It shouldn't have mattered very much, but it did. It was also ironic, Vicars' dismissal had partly hinged on the fact that there were four sets of keys for the strong-room but now, for some unexplained but doubtless embarrassing reason, he had the only set that could be found. Inside the strong-room were a number of the insignia that were necessary for the forthcoming state functions. It was traditional at such functions for the Lord Lieutenant to carry the Sword of State and for him to be preceded by two mace bearers. All three objects were locked in the strong-room.

Were Aberdeen to appear without this paraphernalia, questions would be asked. The answers would put Vicars back centre stage and so some way had to be found of getting the remaining regalia out of the strong-room.

Fate obviously dictated that, at some time, for some reason, the wall of the strong-room was going to be demolished. Four years earlier, Vicars' decision to leave the safe in the library had saved Pemberton the trouble of having to smash his creation himself, but now it had to go – the only way in was by removing the bricks. The conspirators chose Sunday 2nd February to do the deed, bargaining that the vigilance of the press corps would be more relaxed on a Sunday.

Assembled in the Bedford Tower to do the job were three men from the Board of Works – Doran and Conway, who were stone-masons, and Bent, who was a fitter and who had grappled with the strong-room before. He was one of the contingent that had spent a frustrating day in April 1903 trying to squeeze the safe through the strong-room door. Each man was armed with a pick-axe, Doran and Conway also carried hammers and chisels. The messenger's room was overflowing with 'observers' from the DMP, the Board of Works and just about every other State body except the Congested Districts Board. In view of the crush, a representative from that agency would have been equally appropriate.

The workmen set to. The audience, having observed, began to dwindle. After a couple of hours of strenuous percussion, it became apparent that the wall was not going to surrender easily. Pemberton had done his job well. A hole, of sorts, eventually appeared. Those left standing about considered the situation. It would take hours to create a hole big enough to allow a man to get through. A child was the obvious solution, but would they get one who could keep a secret?

Bent offered a solution, he had a fifteen-year-old son, Jack, small for his age, who worked with him as an apprentice and could be relied upon to keep his mouth shut. The lad was sent for and he came, reluctantly. He had been about to begin a game of football and only agreed to the job when he was offered overtime.

The work continued, becoming less feverish as time went on. The ever-decreasing group of observers covered their eyes and noses against the mortar dust being sent up in huge clouds by the pickaxes. Finally, an opening appeared big enough to allow Jack Bent access. The apprentice fitter crawled through. Once inside, he passed out the Sword of State, the maces and, most importantly, whatever keys he could find in the drawers of the strong-room. The job was finally finished at eight o'clock on Monday morning, Jack Bent received 1/6d (9 cent) for his trouble. If Vicars was hoping to infuriate his former associates in Dublin Castle, he was going about it the right way.

On 17th February 1908, the event most feared by Shackleton during the inquiry took place. The 'Blue Book of Evidence' taken by the commission was published. For a brief moment, it brought the case into the limelight again. The London *Times* printed much of the evidence and summarised even more. To Shackleton's undoubted chagrin, the printed transcripts concentrated on his evidence. What he had had to say was, after all, the most newsworthy. The publication of the minutes of the inquiry had the desired effect. The few remaining whimpers from the press demanding fair play for Vicars became almost inaudible.

But Pierce O'Mahony's voice had not been silenced. He had yet to exhaust the defence of his half-brother. He returned to the fray in March 1908 with a spirited rebuttal to criticisms of Vicars made in the *London Opinion* magazine by a romantic novelist of the day, Marie Corelli. He struck a few glancing blows at the author before concentrating his best swipes on the political reputation and character of Augustine Birrell. Firstly, he accused him of being 'absolutely devoid of what are supposed to be the feelings of an English gentleman'. He really cut loose towards the end of his piece. He had already accused the police of withholding evidence that was favourable to his brother. 'I now go further,' he added. 'I state deliberately that the government does not wish to find the thief because one suspected man and one of his associates, also suspected, are known to the police as men of unclean lives, and have threatened to involve society in an unsavoury scandal... a few titled members of what is so falsely called the "Upper Ten" and who circle round the throne, possess characters so absolutely rotten and degraded that they fear to face the threats of two men whom the Rt Hon A Birrell has described as "abandoned ruffians".'

It was O'Mahony's most acerbic public statement to date, and he was not a man to mince words at any time. As far as O'Mahony was concerned, the campaign to vindicate Vicars had not ended with the publication of the findings of the Crown Jewels commission – it had merely entered a new phase. Neither was it to consist of sniping from the sidelines in the form of letters to the press or occasional articles like the one for the *London Opinion*. The real fight was being brought to Westminster.

Laurence Ginnell was not a popular man within his own party. He was too outspoken and pugnacious even for an organisation that had produced many firebrands in its history. He liked to stir things up and to provoke the government but, in doing so, he frequently embarrassed his own colleagues as well. Not that that concerned him, as long as he was popular with the small farmers who elected him. He reckoned his constituents enjoyed the idea of their MP making the likes of the Chief Secretary squirm and some were not unhappy to see him make his leader John Redmond uncomfortable as well. The Irish Parliamentary Party chief was altogether too cosy with the Liberal administration for the liking of many.

Ginnell was the Irish nationalist MP for Westmeath. However, to use a phrase later popularised by Éamon de Valera, he was only 'slightly constitutional'. He was suspected of involvement in the agrarian crime of cattle driving, a practice that was widespread in Ireland at the time. British land-purchase measures had whetted the Irish appetite for peasant proprietorship, however, the pace of land reform was slow, much to the annoyance of Irish farmers who were also irked by the unwillingness of certain landlords to sell out. Birrell's major contribution to his Irish brief had come through his efforts to increase the level of Irish tenant purchases. Cattle driving was an impediment to this process. In itself, it was not such a serious crime. As the name suggests, a man, usually a landlord, who was proving obdurate and immovable, might wake up one morning to find his cattle miles away from his farm. Their exertions on the journey there and back were not calculated to increase their value. Ginnell was suspected of organising cattle drives but not enough proof was ever obtained to charge him with direct involvement.

Although not an inspired parliamentarian, Ginnell made quite an impression within the confines of the House of Commons. However, it was not for his ringing oratory that he was famous. He chose Question Time as his personal battlefield and delighted in making a nuisance of himself. Birrell once described him, in a letter to Prime Minister Campbell Bannerman, as 'that pestilent ass Ginnell, a solitary, unpopular fellow, a very bad speaker of no personal influence, hated by his own party, but a clever writer'.

There was too much of the feisty peasant about Ginnell for him ever to have accepted the gentlemanly conventions of the Houses of Parliament. Ultimately, he took, what was for him, the only logical step. He resigned from the Nationalist Party and joined the Republican, abstentionist, Sinn Féin party. He was elected to the First Dáil in the Sinn Féin landslide of 1918 and served, briefly, as their Minister of Propaganda.

Ginnell had nothing in common with Sir Arthur Vicars. But he had plenty in common with Pierce O'Mahony who had also been a nationalist MP. In addition, the Crown Jewels affair was so filled with scandalous details that this *bête noir* of Question Time could use it to inflict some exquisite embarrassment on the government.

He was not the only person to ask questions on the subject of the jewels. But then other queries were often just that, attempts at eliciting information. Ginnell's efforts were more like minor speeches than genuine questions. As far as he was concerned, he knew all the details, all he wanted was confirmation of his (i.e. O'Mahony's) version of the facts from Birrell.

In April 1908, for example, he asked innocently why the crimes found to have been committed in Dublin Castle in 1907 were not included in the statistics of Irish crime for that year. The 'crimes' to which he was referring had nothing to do with the theft of the jewels. He was asking, without actually saying as much, why the incidences of homosexual activity uncovered by the police had been overlooked. They were, after all, indictable offences. Naturally, Birrell denied that any such crimes had ever taken place. It was not the last time Ginnell forced Birrell to bend the truth.

At first, Ginnell approached the whole subject obliquely, gradually introducing more and more detail into his questions and particularly into his supplementary questions. Often the original question was innocent enough, designed to elicit the same ritual, bored denial from Birrell. Then he would follow up with a loaded supplementary, hoping to catch Birrell on the hop.

The most significant exchange between the two politicians took place on 27th April 1909. Ginnell asked his standard question of Birrell. Had he read all the police reports about the theft of the jewels? Did these reports disclose other thefts and other indictable offences and would he 'allow crime committed at the centre of Irish government to escape criminal investigation'?

'The police reports referred to,' replied Birrell guardedly, 'do not disclose any thefts or indictable offences in addition to the theft of the Crown Jewels.'

Ginnell followed up. 'Arising out of both of these questions, is not the Right Honourable Gentleman aware of the evidence of reports — if he has not read them — implicating, as principal and accomplices in theft and also as principals in sodomy and other beastly crimes, F R Shackleton and Captain Gorges?'

The Speaker of the House stirred himself. 'The Honourable Member has really no right to bring in the names of gentlemen in matters of that sort without submitting his question to me. I will say whether it is a proper one to ask.'

But Ginnell had already achieved his objective. He had wanted, for some time, to get the names of Shackleton and Gorges into *Hansard* — the parliamentary record — having been previously prevented from doing so by the vetting procedure that applied to parliamentary questions. He remonstrated with the Speaker anyway, just for the practice.

'On a point of order,' he said. 'I am not allowed to put this question on the paper... Am I allowed to enquire in this House?'

'No,' replied the Speaker, emphatically.

Ginnell could be accused of hiding behind parliamentary privilege (a facility accorded MPs whereby they are protected against the laws of libel for anything said in the chamber). However, Ginnell was to insist later that, if either person mentioned cared to sue, he would waive this right to protection. Neither Shackleton nor Gorges took him up on his offer but, by the same token, Ginnell was never heard to repeat his accusations outside the confines of the House of Commons.

Ginnell continued asking questions about the Crown Jewels

with dogged persistence. Between 1908 and 1913, he put in over twenty separate queries. He had the Chief Secretary on his feet more times on this one topic than all his fellow parliamentarians put together. His most active year was 1913, even though genuine interest in the controversy had died after 1908. The reason for this activity was the enforced return from Portuguese West Africa of Frank Shackleton to face charges of fraud. By the end of that year, Shackleton was a convicted criminal serving a jail sentence and, suddenly, Ginnell's allegations against this apparently honest gentleman didn't seem so far-fetched after all. He repeatedly forced Birrell to be positively miserly with the truth about what the police had uncovered when they were investigating the Crown Jewels theft. He had tricked Birrell into admitting that Inspector Kane's report had named some names, though not necessarily in connection with the theft of the jewels. This, of course, totally discredited Birrell's claims that no crimes, other than the theft of the jewels, had been uncovered.

However, Ginnell was not the only parliamentarian to exploit the possibilities of Question Time, the government itself did so, on more than one occasion, to protect Lord Haddo.

As Shackleton had indicated in his evidence to the commission, he was not the only person to have figured in the rumours that were flying around Dublin about the identity of the thief. The Haddo story originated because he had been identified as Mrs Farrell's mysterious stranger and the fact that he had been out of the country from March to December 1907 didn't stop the stories from spreading.

Lord Aberdeen grew frantic. The logical conclusion to be drawn from such stories was that he was shielding his own son.

In desperation, he consulted MacDonnell, who always tended to tackle problems head on. He suggested that a parliamentary question be planted and that, in the course of the reply, Birrell should refer to the Haddo rumour and refute it absolutely.

On 1st April 1908, Major Coates, Liberal MP for Lewisham, got to his feet and asked Birrell the most innocuous question that MacDonnell had been able to devise. He enquired whether Birrell could state the dates between which the Crown Jewels must have been stolen. Birrell did so with alacrity and, when he had passed on the information requested, added, 'As I am on this subject, I may refer to a most cowardly falsehood connecting the name of Lord Haddo with the theft of the jewels, which has obtained wide circulation both in Dublin and London, and has found its way into certain newspapers. Ridiculous as such a statement may appear, it is not always easy to maintain total indifference to such charges.' He then went on to indicate the dates of Haddo's absence from the country and express the pious wish that this information would put an end to all scandalmongering.

Needless to say, it did no such thing. Those who had not been privy to this juicy piece of gossip were now aware of it. The myth grew. People were prepared to swear they had personally seen Haddo bury the Crown Jewels in the grounds of the Viceregal Lodge in the Phoenix Park. In 1913, there was a resurgence of the rumours about Aberdeen's son when Shackleton re-entered the limelight (for reasons that will be discussed later) and the subject became topical once again.

For the second time, the government went through the motions of issuing a denial. On 5th February 1913, a Captain Faber was due to ask a question that would allow Birrell to scotch the rumours again. At the last moment, he was asked to postpone his question until 13th February. The excuse offered was that Birrell wanted to make an oral reply. That was true enough, but there was a far more compelling reason.

Ginnell had decided to enter the Haddo Stakes himself. He had put down a question for 13th February asking Chief Secretary Birrell: 'What persons, other than officials and their assistants, had access, through relationship and acquaintance with officials and familiarity with the police, to the room in Dublin Castle in which the Crown Jewels were kept at the time those jewels were stolen in 1907?' Birrell's answer was concise and dismissive, 'I know of no such person.'

The file in the State Paper Office relating to the question tells the story behind the cryptic answer. Birrell had hoped to be able to refer to Haddo by name and say that Aberdeen's son had never been in the Office of Arms, officially or unofficially. A wire had been sent, more in hope than expectation, to Sir James Dougherty, to that effect. Dougherty questioned Aberdeen and it emerged, much as had been anticipated, that Haddo had been in the Office of Arms as least once in an official capacity. As a Chamberlain-in-Waiting, he had been sent there, in uniform, with a message from his father.

With that avenue closed off, Birrell decided to opt for the answer that he gave: 'I know of no such person!' But he was determined to broach the subject of Haddo in parliament again and Faber's question was postponed until 13th February to enable him to do so. It would have been obvious to anyone with even the skimpiest grasp of the facts of the case that Ginnell's question referred to Haddo. Birrell didn't want to be seen to duck away from the issue but he wanted to handle it on his own terms, not by means of a barbed question (and potentially dangerous supplementary) from the Westmeath MP.

Faber followed Ginnell and asked, 'Whether now, or at the time of the robbery, information relating to the crime has been available which, for the sake of shielding any individual, has not been used.'

Birrell denied the existence of any cover up. 'The story,' he said, 'which someone must have invented out of spite, that anyone is being shielded from prosecution, is simply a lie; and I am sorry to have to add that it has lately been revived in connection with the name of Lord Haddo. The introduction of his lordship's name into the matter is a particularly cruel outrage, for, as already stated, he was not in Ireland for months before or after the robbery; he had no connection with that office and was only inside that office once in his life.' Birrell sat down, confident that he had nailed the 'lie' once and for all. However, it is still repeated to this day.

In late 1913, political events in Ireland began to catch up with Ginnell, giving him more important things to think about, and he lost interest in the Crown Jewels as a means of needling the government. Not even the conviction of Shackleton for fraud, in October 1913, prompted a question from him. But his obstinate one-man campaign from 1908 to 1913, while not providing many answers, had posed a lot of irksome and embarrassing questions.

At their November 1907 meeting, the republican journalists Joe O'Beirne and Bulmer Hobson had been enthralled by the story that O'Mahony had told them. It confirmed Hobson's suspicion that there was more to the Crown Jewels affair than anyone was prepared to admit and anything that discredited the Dublin Castle administration was grist to his mill. Hobson had got to work immediately. Armed with the information gleaned from O'Mahony, he checked around. He was able to add a few titbits of his own but, when it came to publication, he was wasting his time, something he quickly realised. Nobody would print the story as every paragraph was, potentially, libellous.

This was the main reason why the story was finally published outside the jurisdiction of the British civil courts. A case could still be brought against John Devoy and the New York *Gaelic American* but such an eventuality was unlikely. In addition, because of the American Bill of Rights and the constitutional safeguards of the freedom of the press, the US libel laws were much more liberal than those in Britain. Hobson fully expected to receive a copy of his article within a matter of days of having sent it to Devoy. As it transpired, however, it was weeks before the article was published. Even the normally merciless Devoy had paused before printing it. According to Hobson, the old Fenian found it difficult to believe. By the time the manuscript reached the front page of the *Gaelic American*, it had been severely edited. The most significant change was in the references to Gorges, for some unknown reason, Devoy had changed the name and Gorges became 'Gaudeons'. Shackleton, however, remained plain Shackleton.

Thus amended, the story appeared on 4th July 1908. Even though he may not have had total confidence in it, Devoy gave it the full treatment. There was nothing subtle or understated about the phraseology: 'ABOMINATIONS OF DUBLIN CASTLE EXPOSED' ran the screaming banner headline, across three columns. The subheading told the whole story:

> *Mystery of the Theft of the Crown Jewels Brought to Light – Gang of Aristocratic Degenerates Carried on Their Orgies in the Citadel of British Rule and the Thieves Were Among Them – Sir Arthur Vicars Made a Scapegoat to Screen Lord Haddo, Son of Lord Aberdeen, and the Duke of Argyle [sic], King Edward's Son-in-Law – John Redmond Helped to Hush Up the Infamy to Oblige His Friend Birrell and the Liberal Government That Has Slammed the Door on Home Rule – A Dark Chapter in the History of Cork Hill.*

Only the humble articles, conjunctions and prepositions were deemed unworthy of capital letters.

In the article, Vicars was cast in the role of scapegoat abused by Aberdeen, Birrell and King Edward VII, all of whom had helped hush up the scandal. 'But,' screamed Devoy, 'the incident is not closed. They may silence every voice in Ireland, but they cannot silence the *Gaelic American*. We will see to it that the whole rottenness and infamy of the English government in Ireland is published to the world.' Shackleton came in for particular vilification. Unknown to Vicars, the article claimed, when he had introduced Shackleton into the Office of Arms the man: '...was well known to the police. Around his name had gathered a lot of very unsavoury rumours. Some of his associates, titled and untitled, were men suspected of unspeakable and disgusting offences… the English police had a record of his career at Scotland Yard.'

Devoy and Hobson then railed against the 'nightly orgies' in Dublin Castle, where the guests included Shackleton, Haddo, Sir John Mille Goldsmith ('head of the English secret police in Ireland') and Gaudeons. The orgies took place in the Bedford Tower, but always, according to Hobson, loyal to his source, after the virtuous Sir Arthur Vicars had returned home. 'So things went on till one fine day it was discovered that the jewels were gone. Who stole them we can surmise.' The article then goes on to do just that – exposing Shackleton and Gaudeons as the criminals.

The role of Scotland Yard was also alluded to. The *Gaelic American* referred to the arrival, from London, of 'several detectives'. 'After a few days they unravelled the mystery and the case was promptly taken out of their hands. The Scotland Yard men found out too much and were sent home at once. To find out more than is wanted is a very bad thing for a detective to do in a case of this sort.' The paper then explains why Shackleton and/or Gaudeons were allowed to get away with their crime. The cover-up was because of Shackleton's connection with the Duke of Argyll, the King's brother-in-law. According to the *Gaelic American*, he was 'a man of very bad reputation to say the least of it, and it is to shield such "abandoned aristocratic ruffians" that a public inquiry was refused, and that the men who stole the jewels were allowed by the police to escape. If Shackleton and Gaudeons were arrested they could tell a story about their titled associates that would make Edward VII blush.'

The article has many factual inaccuracies though these are usually of a minor nature. But, despite Devoy's editing, Hobson's story (with O'Mahony as his main source) remains substantially intact, and largely unverifiable. The article, sensational allegations aside, is little more than an apologia for Sir Arthur Vicars. It was the only occasion on which the claims of the Vicars faction got such a public, uncompromising airing. But what Devoy and Hobson presented as facts were very often informed guesses or opinions born of the prejudice of their sources.

Devoy's conviction that the criminals had now been uncovered was not shared by the police. They still professed to be baffled more than a year after the crime had been committed. In September 1908, Harrell was asked by Aberdeen to supply him with a report on any progress that might have occurred in the investigations. Harrel's summary of the advances that had been made, communicated through Dougherty, was short and must have made depressing reading for Aberdeen. In essence, it was an admission of total failure, the police had nowhere to go. Harrel's assessment was stark and honest. 'I regret to say,' he wrote, 'that the police are still without any clue and there is, therefore, no immediate prospect of success attending their efforts which have been continuous and zealous.'

The police had followed up every possible lead, they had pursued enquiries in England and even in America. They could not even say whether the jewels were intact or had long since been broken up. Harrel was not optimistic of their ever finding out. He had been led to believe by Vicars and others that, at the time of the theft, the collection would have been difficult to dispose of. He no longer believed that. Experts had told him that, out of their settings, the gems would not be recognised.

Two lines of Harrel's report stand out: 'Two of the persons

connected with the case, who are resident in Ireland, on whom suspicion rested somewhat strongly, have, if guilty, derived no immediate benefit from the proceeds of the crime.' The reference could be to Shackleton and Gorges, however, neither could, properly, be said to be permanently resident in Ireland. On the other hand, the only two men connected with the case who were resident in Ireland were Vicars and Pierce Gun Mahony. At no stage was either man seriously under suspicion.

Harrel made a ritual assurance that Aberdeen could have absolute confidence that the vigilance of the DMP 'will be in no way relaxed'. It was suitably gung ho, but more realistic was his observation that 'there are still some points for further enquiry, but I am not sanguine that they will lead to anything tangible'. You didn't have to read between the lines to realise what he was saying. The police investigation was over and, short of tripping themselves up, the thieves were home free.

Act Three

Denouement

9

Death and Misadventure

'…*the Dreyfus of the case, Sir Arthur Vicars, is left by the Government on his Devil's Island, and nemesis has overtaken several persons whose names were prominently mentioned during the so-called trial.*'

John Bull, 1911

A SUPERSTITION HAS grown up around the legendary Hope Diamond. It is said that whoever possesses the stone will meet with ill luck. The same is true of the treasure of the Egyptian Boy King, Tutankhamun. It is as if there is something intrinsic within the objects themselves that is evil and which radiates that evil.

The stones that made up the Irish Crown Jewels have no such myths built up around them. Those that originally belonged to King George IV had a sordid rather than melodramatic history. So, presumably, it is merely a coincidence that four of the men whose names have been mentioned extensively in connection with the theft of the jewels met with varying degrees of bad fortune within a matter of years.

Two were to die violent deaths, while the other two were to go to jail.

Pierce Gun Mahony had emerged unscathed from the turmoil of the theft and its aftermath. He had not been asked to resign and he was constantly referred to, in correspondence between Dublin and London, as the only innocent who would suffer in the round of dismissals. Had the unsentimental MacDonnell had his way, Mahony would have been sacked along with Vicars, Shackleton and Goldney. It was the intervention of Lord Aberdeen that prolonged the agony of Vicars and saved Mahony, who remained at the Office of Arms for the next three years.

In 1910, Mahony resigned as Cork Herald, as he had been called to the Bar. At around that time, he moved from his home in Burlington Road in Dublin to a house belonging to his father in Castleisland, County Kerry. (Vicars was staying nearby and was a frequent visitor.)

In July 1914, Mahony paid his father a visit at the family home in Grange Con, County Wicklow. Europe was on the verge of war and the focus of any conflict looked like being the Balkans. Pierce O'Mahony was depressed by what he saw was about to happen to a part of the world he loved. His son was less concerned with such matters, he had never shared his father's romantic attachment to the Balkans, neither was he gripped by the uncertainty that was affecting those ten to fifteen years his junior. If there was to be a war, he was past the age where he might have been expected to enlist automatically. So Mahony could enjoy the fine summer weather in the idyllic surroundings of his father's elegant demesne. On the evening of Sunday 27th July, he was invited to join a group of friends for some shooting on an adjoining estate. He decided to row across the lake that divided the two holdings. He loaded his shotgun and walked down to the boathouse. He left, saying he would be back well before dark.

He wasn't missed until much later that evening. Pierce O'Mahony began to worry slightly and sent Athanas Blagoff, a Bulgarian refugee who was staying with the family, down to the boathouse to see had the boat been returned. Blagoff found it, tied up. Although he did not know it at the time, the boat had never been moved.

Blagoff now became concerned himself. He decided to wander along the shore of the lake to see if he could spot Mahony. He had not gone far before he noticed a body, floating in the reeds. He dashed into the water and grabbed it but there was no sign of life. Quickly, he waded back to shore with the corpse. As he placed Mahony on the ground, he saw immediately what had happened. The man had not drowned, he had no chest left. It had been shot away.

The inquest on Mahony brought in a verdict of accidental death. The shotgun was found near a barbed wire fence beside the boathouse. It was assumed that Mahony had climbed this and had then lifted the gun after him. The trigger had caught in the barbed wire and both barrels had gone off. It was stated at the inquest that the injuries received could not have been self-inflicted. This is a charitable but, on the face of it, improbable assessment as it is far easier to shoot yourself in the chest than it is to snag your trigger on some barbed wire and have that do the job for you. This is not to suggest that Mahony did commit suicide, only that he could have. He could just as easily have been shot by 'a person or persons unknown'.

Mahony was not the only person to die violently that weekend. In Bachelor's Walk, Dublin, three people had been killed and thirty-eight wounded by the King's Own Scottish Borderers in the aftermath of the successful landing of arms for the Irish Volunteers by Erskine Childers from the yacht *Asgard* in Howth Harbour. On their return to barracks, passing along the north Liffey quays, the soldiers had been barracked unmercifully by a mob. No one really knows what started the shooting, but the results were tragic.

The Assistant Commissioner for the Dublin Metropolitan Police, M V Harrel, was not on the scene at the time. Neither had he any direct control over the King's Own Scottish Borderers. There were calls for the resignation of the Under Secretary, James Brown Dougherty. But he did what he had done as MacDonnell's assistant, he kept his head down and clung on. Still, three people had died and someone had to be thrown to the wolves. Harrel was chosen. He was not protected by his years of service and his career ended ignominiously, in much the same manner as that of Vicars.

'Retired Officer Charged with Murder' – The Times, 16th July 1915

Captain Richard Howard Gorges suited the army and the army suited him. He had a streak of viciousness that, when properly harnessed, was useful in war. The officers of the South African Cape Mounted Police, of which he was a valued member, were not avuncular guardians of the law. They were tough and often callous, operating, as they did, in a hostile environment, dividing their time between rebellious natives and sullen Dutch farmers.

A soldier serving in South Africa had three great fears: spears, disease and the sun. Gorges fell victim to the third of these. He suffered an immobilising bout of sunstroke in the Matabele War of 1896, the effects of which would never leave him. One of his commanding officers in that war, a Major Ritchie, thought highly of Gorges' qualities as a soldier. When he came across him again during the Boer War (1899–1902), Ritchie noted that Gorges had changed completely. The fearlessness and rage were still there but now they were proving more difficult to control. His frequent recourse to alcohol to deaden his excruciating headaches made his behaviour even more violent and unpredictable.

Gorges emerged from the Boer War a much-decorated man, awarded a Queen's Medal with five clasps and a King's Medal with two clasps. Had the empire provided a succession of wars for him to fight, all might have been well with Gorges. Instead, after the Boer War, he was sent back to England and became a captain in the 3rd Battalion of the Royal Irish Regiment, based in Portsmouth. In 1904, he was appointed Regimental Musketry Instructor and from then on divided his time between Portsmouth and Ireland.

Gorges' friendship with Shackleton, which began in 1905, had been frowned upon by Vicars. For a year, Sir Arthur had tolerated the erratic captain's visits to Clonskeagh but he considered him 'morally a bad lot' and was not about to be made feel uncomfortable by anyone in his own home. He issued an ultimatum to Shackleton in 1906, banning Gorges from the house and the latter didn't bother to argue – he knew he would be spending very little time in Dublin that year. Gorges did not visit the house in Clonskeagh again.

The peacetime army and Gorges found it difficult to adapt to one another. Gorges' behaviour became increasingly unpredictable and the army lost patience with him. They parted company in 1908.

Gorges drifted, wandering from one small London 'hotel' or rooming house to another. He drank consistently and spent most of the time close to out-and-out destitution. In 1911, he appeared in court for defrauding the lady proprietor of a West Kensington Hotel of £4 and of getting lodgings without paying. The regiment rallied round, in purse if not in person, and the money was paid back. At the hearing, a number of testimonials were produced pointing out the service that Gorges had rendered his country and itemising the wounds and medals he had received. He got a sympathetic judge and was bound over.

He then decided to try his luck in Ireland. He came with something to sell. It was an idea born of bitterness and experience. The bitterness was against the army and the authorities, the experience was the knowledge he had gained of the security arrangements of Dublin Castle.

Sometime in 1912, Bulmer Hobson was at work in the offices of a journal he edited called *Irish Freedom*. With him was a man called Jocelyn O'Hehir who had brought Hobson several articles that he intended to print. In the course of the conversation, O'Hehir mentioned that he had bumped into Gorges, an old acquaintance, and that, furthermore, the ex-soldier was interested in contacting Hobson.

Hobson recognised the name instantly, but he was suspicious. He did not know O'Hehir all that well and wondered if he was being led into some sort of trap. 'Who is Gorges?' he asked, disingenuously.

'Well,' said O'Hehir, 'when I was a boy I knew him, and he has been abroad and I had not seen him since, till I met him a couple of days ago.'

Hobson studied O'Hehir closely and decided the younger man was telling the truth. He was intrigued. What could Gorges want with him? It was four years since he had written the article for the *Gaelic American*. Was it conceivable that Gorges could have read the article, discovered the identity of the author and was now intent on extracting his revenge? He thought it highly unlikely, doubting that Gorges would ever even have seen the offending piece. He told O'Hehir to send Gorges to the offices of *Irish Freedom* in D'Olier Street the following afternoon.

He then contacted a friend, asked him to take the afternoon off work and wait in an adjoining office, just in case. Hobson wanted to hear whatever it was the captain had to say, but he had gleaned something of the man's reputation for violent behaviour from O'Mahony.

The following afternoon Gorges arrived. In his autobiography, Hobson describes him as a 'tall military figure, with a face like Mephistopheles in *Faust*, and manners that a Duke might envy'.

Hobson felt secure, with help only a few yards away, and decided to get straight to the point, not waiting to find out why the ex-soldier had come.

'You know, Captain Gorges,' he said, 'your name seems familiar.'

'Oh,' replied Gorges, 'that's odd.'

'I think I saw something about you in an American newspaper recently. In fact, I think I have a copy of the paper here.'

With that Hobson, by his own account, handed Gorges a copy of the 4th July 1908 edition of the *Gaelic American*.

This is where Hobson's version of events shows a major inconsistency. According to him, Gorges read a few paragraphs, then jumped from his seat and read the rest of the article pacing the room like a caged tiger. 'My God,' he muttered. 'If I knew who wrote that I would murder him.'

The problem with Hobson's account is that the story in the *Gaelic American* had been doctored by Devoy, so that Gorges had become 'Gaudeons'. Accordingly, there was no reason for anyone other than the writer of the piece to suspect that the person referred to as Gaudeons was in fact Captain Gorges. Gorges was also no fool, and it surely would not have taken him long to realise that he was addressing the author of the article.

Hobson makes no attempt to explain the inconsistency. He does not seem to have even been aware of it. It doesn't totally discredit his account of the meeting, but it plants some doubts at the very least.

According to Hobson, once Gorges had calmed down, he proceeded, unasked, to confirm the contents of the story. He even explained the reason for the rumours about Haddo – that he had taken the jewels one night, after a particularly drunken party, but had returned them the next day. Shackleton and Gorges had been witnesses. The ease with which the jewels had been 'stolen' had given them the idea for the robbery.

But that was not what Gorges had come to discuss. It was getting late by the time the two men finished talking about the theft of the jewels. Gorges asked Hobson to join him for dinner in Jury's Hotel on Dame Street. Hobson was disinclined to allow himself to be seen in public with Gorges. He turned down the invitation, but Gorges pressed him. Finally, Hobson agreed to meet him the next day in Jury's.

When they met again, Gorges wanted to adjourn to a private room. Hobson was still wary of the unpredictable nature of the other man's temper and so edged him towards a large tearoom where it was public and relatively safe.

Over tea, Gorges unfolded his scheme, one that astonished Hobson. The man who had served in the British army since he was a callow youth now wanted to assist militant Republicans in carrying out an insurrection. What's more, he insisted that he had a plan that would help such an enterprise succeed. Hobson's puzzlement grew as the man outlined his scheme.

It was based on the idea of a surprise assault on every army barracks in Dublin. On Sunday mornings, each garrison was marched out on church parade carrying only sidearms and leaving only a few men in barracks. It would take, he calculated, about one hundred men to secure every barracks in the city. Once this was achieved, the rebels would be inside with arms and ammunition and the regular soldiers would be outside with useless sidearms. It was an outrageous and daring plan.

As he listened, Hobson became absolutely convinced of one

thing, this was a blatant attempt at entrapment. Gorges was an *agent provocateur* sent by the authorities, either to infiltrate the Republican movement or to enlist certain members of that movement in an indictable conspiracy. In addition, Hobson was unimpressed by the plan, therefore he had no reason to express any great enthusiasm.

He decided to bluff his way out of the situation and interrupted Gorges in full flight. 'Captain Gorges,' he said. 'I don't think you realise that all this talk of rebellion in Ireland is just talk. Your plan sounds an excellent one and, if it were a surprise attack, might well succeed, but you must face the fact that these fellows who talk about an insurrection and Irish freedom don't mean a single thing. You could not get ten men for such an enterprise.'

Gorges was crestfallen and, though he argued with Hobson a while longer, the latter was adamant. There would be no rebellion because there was no stomach for it. Hobson stuck to his guns all the way to the front door of Jury's.

Gorges may well have been an *agent provocateur* but, given his recent relationship with the army, it is most unlikely. It is more probable that he hoped to restore his fortunes by acting on his own initiative in infiltrating the Republican movement and/or the emerging Irish Volunteer organisation. He may have hoped to enlist the support of the more extreme faction of that force for his plan and then turn them over to Dublin Castle. It would have been his ticket back into the army.

It was two years before he did, eventually, work his way back into the forces, though, predictably he was needed only because of a new war, the one that was supposed to 'end all wars'. Even then, his recall came about only because service records were ignored in the scramble to beef up the British Expeditionary Force in the autumn of 1914.

Gorges slipped into the wartime army with the rank of captain but lasted only a few months. His aggressive qualities would not have suited the stagnant war of attrition being fought in the trenches by the winter of 1914. In January 1915, he was allowed to resign his commission and he returned to the rooming houses of London, disillusioned and apparently worthless. Soldiering was all he had ever known, but, even in an army desperate for manpower, his services were surplus to requirements.

On 2nd June 1915, he rented two rooms in Mount Vernon in Hampstead. The house where he was staying was owned by a man called Caraher, a former policeman. With women in the streets handing out white feathers to men of fighting age not in uniform, Gorges felt the need to explain why he wasn't at the front. He invented a cover story, which he told to anyone who would listen, that he had been invalided home after being gassed in France. He was now unfit for active service. At least the latter part of his story was true.

Gorges now occupied his time by drinking. His staple was brandy and ginger ale but, when he was low on funds, he would drink stout. Whatever he drank, he downed in vast quantities, having developed a high tolerance for alcohol over the years. The amount he was able to consume would have flattened most men but left him, to all appearances, sober. He soon became well known around Hampstead.

Gorges had been going to seed for some time and his Hampstead sojourn accelerated that process. Before moving to the

Caraher house, he had visited a GP, Dr Seymour, in Hampstead. His headaches were becoming unbearable and he appealed to the doctor for help. The haggard appearance and the uncontrollable shake in the hand of this shell of a man told Seymour all he needed to know. He diagnosed acute alcoholism. This was of scarce comfort to Gorges. He had one remedy for all his ills and did not want to be deprived of it. He continued to drink.

One of Gorges' associates in Hampstead was Charles Thoroughgood, an aspiring boxer. However, Thoroughgood quickly tired of his new-found acquaintance. Gorges' belligerence particularly irritated him. On one occasion, when the boxer warned him that his violent language and behaviour would get him in trouble with the police, Gorges shouted at him, 'I'll shoot stone dead the first one that lays a hand on me.' He illustrated his intentions graphically by waving at Thoroughgood the revolver he kept in his hip pocket.

The nights were the worst time for Gorges. The drinking had to end sometime and he would return to his rooms after closing time. Occasionally, whatever alcoholic mist he had been able to generate would clear before he fell asleep and he would have to face the night without his customary crutch. Sometimes, on those nights, his own black depression would infuriate him. He would pick up one of the two service revolvers he still kept with him and loose off a volley of shots out his bedroom window into the darkness beyond.

That was what alerted the police. They began to get complaints about Gorges' nocturnal shootouts and two detectives were sent to investigate.

Detectives Askew and Young turned up on Mrs Caraher's doorstep early on the morning of 14th July 1915. They asked to see Gorges and, when they were told that he was not in, they requested permission to examine his rooms. Mrs Caraher did not object and showed them upstairs. They left shortly afterwards, taking with them one of Gorges' service revolvers and 197 cartridges. They should have been alerted by the fact that the ammunition was of two different types – so Gorges was still carrying his other revolver, a Smith and Wesson .39. They talked to Mrs Caraher before they left and asked her not to tell Gorges what had happened if he missed the gun.

At eight thirty that evening, Gorges returned to the house. He had been drinking heavily and he was accompanied by another acquaintance, known as Muncer. The two men went upstairs but Gorges was back down within minutes. He began to shout at Mrs Caraher, loudly accusing her husband of having stolen the gun, the ammunition and a watch. Mrs Caraher protested her husband's innocence.

At nine fifty, the two policemen returned. Gorges was in the basement and Mrs Caraher showed them down. They met the lodger on the steps. Askew and Young asked him to take them up to his room, they wanted to talk to him 'man to man'. He agreed, but insisted they both go on ahead and he would follow. Young demurred, he asked Gorges to lead the way.

'Am I under arrest?' Gorges enquired, as they walked upstairs.

'Yes,' replied Young.

Askew was watching Gorges closely all the time. He noticed the man fumble behind his back.

'What have you got in your pockets?' he asked.

'That is my business,' Gorges snarled.

Then, without warning, he produced the Smith and Wesson

and aimed it at Detective Young. Askew moved quickly, diving at Gorges' right arm in an attempt to knock away the gun. He missed and, instead, pinned Gorges' left arm to the wall. Gorges was able to shoot and he hit Young from a distance of just over a foot. The policeman tumbled down the stairs clutching his chest.

Askew was left to fight for his own life. He was unarmed and, wisely, did not loosen the grip he had on Gorges.

'Let me go, you bastard,' shouted Gorges. 'I'll give you something.'

Askew managed to plant both his feet on Gorges' body and pushed him forward with all his strength. Gorges overbalanced and fell, his head hitting the banisters and breaking two of the rails. He dropped the gun.

The shot had aroused the house and help arrived. Mr Caraher and Jameson, another lodger, came racing down the stairs. As Askew grabbed the revolver, he screamed at Jameson to sit on Gorges' head. The older and less mobile Caraher contented himself with gripping firmly the middle fingers of Gorges' left hand. Afterwards, he was to boast that 'once I get hold, no man can let me go'.

Askew now had the gun. Gorges continued to struggle but knew that he was beaten. The detective backed down the stairs, never taking his eyes off his assailant. When he got to the bottom, he leaned over his colleague seeing at once that he was dead.

In custody that night, Gorges alternated between remorse and bravado. To one policeman, he expressed regret at Young's death, insisting that he had not meant to kill him. But by five o'clock in the morning, his native truculence had reasserted itself. He asked a guard in the cells how many policemen there were in

Hampstead. On being told there were fifty, he replied, 'Well, I had enough rounds for them all.'

At Hampstead Police Court later that morning, his mood had swung back again. He was charged with the wilful murder of Detective Young and pleaded not guilty.

'I wish to say that I did it accidentally,' he told the judge. 'It was his fault for having tried to take the revolver from me. I had no more intention of shooting him than of shooting you. I was in liquor.'

He was a pathetic sight but, even in his extremity, he still clung to one absolute. He virtually begged not to be charged as 'Captain' Gorges. 'Don't call me captain,' he pleaded. 'For the sake of the regiment.' The police were unsympathetic.

The inquest into Young's death took place on 27th July. An attempt was made to introduce Gorges' medical history in evidence, but the coroner was firm in his instructions to the jury. Sunstroke or no sunstroke, it was not within the competence of a coroner's jury to consider questions of sanity. The outcome was predictable. Young was adjudged to have died of injuries received from Gorges' bullet and the verdict was wilful murder.

At his trial in September 1915, Gorges' character witnesses had almost completely deserted him. Only the obliging Major Ritchie, at the request of the defence counsel, testified to the defendant's excellence as a soldier in the Matabele War and the unfortunate change that the sunstroke had brought about in his character. Dr Seymour was brought in to tell the jury of Gorges' alcoholism. The line of defence was to establish diminished responsibility and it succeeded. Gorges escaped the hangman's noose. He was found guilty of manslaughter and sentenced to twelve years penal servitude.

Gorges makes one final incursion into this story, just over a year later. In December 1916, Scotland Yard received reports of a very peculiar kind. It appeared that an inmate of one of His Majesty's prisons had passed on some information about his cellmate, who was in the habit of regaling him with the story of how he had stolen the Irish Crown Jewels. Naturally, the convict dismissed the claims of his eccentric and possibly deranged cellmate, but decided to report them anyway.

Scotland Yard, however, was more interested because the cellmate was Gorges. The police would have liked to despatch the estimable Inspector John Kane to investigate, however he had died the previous year, aged sixty-two. Instead, a former colleague of Kane's, Inspector Sanders, who had assisted Kane in the original inquiry, was sent to look into the matter. Maddeningly, all that is known about that meeting between Sanders and Gorges is that the inspector incurred expenses of £7.13.7 in the course of his duty.

Of all those involved in the Crown Jewels affair, Gorges was the most aggressive, violent and unpredictable. He had lengthened the odds on his own longevity by the amount of alcohol he consumed and the active military service he saw. He was extremely lucky to have escaped hanging. Therefore, it is ironic that he outlived all the others who were touched by the robbery and its aftermath. When he died in the 1960s, Richard Howard Gorges was well into his nineties.

'End of the Shackleton Case – Defendants Found Guilty' – *The Times,* 25th October 1913

For Francis Shackleton, the Mexican Land and Timber Company was to be his meal ticket for life – if the investment paid off, he stood to make over £70,000. The scheme was a simple one involving the purchase of a vast tract of land in Mexico that would then be exploited for the huge quantities of timber it would provide. If the capital could be found to fund the investment, there was a small fortune to be made.

Shackleton's other business enterprises were sidelines compared to the scale of the Land and Timber Company but, in a sense, they were all feeding into it. Because of his involvement, three other companies were tied into the Central American land deal: the Celtic Investment Trust Company; the grandiosely named International Finance and Development Corporation; and the Montevideo Public Works Corporation, which was, in theory at least, attempting to raise money to build a major jetty in the Uruguayan capital.

In addition to his own affairs, Shackleton was also in demand as a sort of informal business manager for some of his friends. Lord Ronald Sutherland Gower was particularly reliant upon him. Gower, an artist and aesthete, lacked any knowledge of financial matters. For years, he had enjoyed an annual income of £1,500, derived from holdings of £40,000 in railway shares. Then, in 1907, his financial adviser died and Shackleton stepped in.

Power of attorney was signed over to an associate of Shackleton's, a chartered accountant, Thomas Jehu Garlick.

Through Shackleton's intercession, Garlick was also granted power of attorney over the business affairs of Gower's adopted son Frank Hird and a friend of theirs, Miss Josephine Browne. Shackleton had first met Miss Browne in Gower's house in Penshurst in 1906 where she had been impressed by his charm and suavity. She grew extremely fond of him and invited him to visit her at her home in Tavistock in Kent in 1907.

On that visit, Shackleton, in the guise of a disinterested honest broker, brought up the subject of Miss Browne's investments. He tut-tutted when he heard her money was in Lloyd's Bank and railway shares. He warned her, solemnly, that he himself would never stand over such a portfolio. The Lloyd's Bank shares had not been fully paid for and Miss Browne risked losing them completely if the bank insisted that the unpaid capital of £18,000 be handed over. As for the railway shares, he pointed to the ominous rise in the popularity of the motor car as an indication that the days of the railway were past. In October of that year, the ubiquitous Garlick was given power of attorney over Miss Browne's finances.

Shackleton and Garlick began, systematically, to abuse the financial control they had been given and, within five years, left Gower, Hird and Miss Browne virtually penniless.

In December 1907, Gower's railway stock was sold off and, in return, he received 40,000 £1 shares in the International Finance and Development Corporation. From time to time, he received dividends from his investment, however, these dividends were not the proceeds of profits earned by the company, but were simply paid out of his original capital to deceive Gower into thinking that his investment was paying off handsomely.

This was also the case with Hird and Miss Browne. Both had a considerable amount of money invested in Celtic and International shares – Hird handed over £12,500, while Miss Browne cashed in her Lloyd's Bank and railway shares, which realised about £12,000. This was passed on to Shackleton to use to her best advantage. In reality, her money was being sunk into the two companies and disappearing without trace in pursuit of the Mexican El Dorado.

Over the Christmas and New Year period of 1909 to 1910, Gower, Hird and Miss Browne stayed at Gower's Penshurst residence where Shackleton was an occasional visitor. On one of his stays there, Miss Browne began to wonder aloud when she would receive an inheritance, amounting to £1,000, that was due to her. Shackleton became very attentive at the mention of this sum of money. 'Whenever you get it,' he said, 'let me have it. I will invest it for you in something good.'

The following February, Miss Browne did indeed send the bequest cheque to Shackleton. She asked him to invest it for her. Instead of doing this, he lodged it to his own account in Cox's Bank. By 1910, with the constant need to top up his investment in the Mexican land deal, he had built up an overdraft at Cox's of £40,000. The overdraft was secured by a signed guarantee from Gower and 60,000 £1 shares in the Montevideo Public Works Corporation. As it happened, these shares were totally valueless – a fact of which Shackleton was only too well aware.

The bank was pressurising Shackleton to clear off his huge debt, while the stockbrokers representing him in the Mexican enterprise were looking for more money to secure that crucial investment. Shackleton needed cash quickly and succeeded in persuading Gower to hand over £5,000 (on the understanding that it was to purchase 5,000 shares in the Montevideo Public Works Corporation). Gower was completely unaware of the fact that he already had 40,000 shares in this company and Shackleton didn't enlighten him. He was, therefore, honest with Gower about the purpose for which the money was intended. However, there was more to it than just the straightforward purchase of 5,000 shares – it was all part of a fraudulent ruse devised by Shackleton.

The scheme was put into effect just in time. Cox's Bank was beginning to have doubts about the value of the £60,000 worth of Montevideo shares that were the part guarantee of Shackleton's massive overdraft. They wanted some money from their heavily indebted customer, and they wanted to obtain this money by making Shackleton test the market for the Montevideo shares by selling off some of his portfolio in that concern. They suggested that he offload £10,000 worth to begin with. However, not even the eminently plausible Shackleton could find any legitimate buyers – but he had to convince the bank that the shares had some value.

Shackleton, however, had it figured out. He approached a stockbroking firm called Rowe & Pitman and engaged their services to buy 5,000 shares in the Montevideo Public Works Corporation for Gower. Furthermore, Rowe & Pitman were told that they were to buy the 5,000 Montevideo shares from one firm and one firm only, the brokers Linton, Clarke & Company. They were not to bargain with them either, but simply buy the shares at face value and take their commission.

What Shackleton knew was that Linton, Clarke & Company were the stockbrokers representing Cox's Bank. They were instructed by the bank to sell 5,000 Montevideo shares belonging to Shackleton and when Shackleton was consulted, he suggested they try and sell them to Rowe & Pitman, he had heard they were very interested. On 1st March 1910, the deal was done on the floor of the Stock Exchange between the two brokerage companies. Five thousand Montevideo Public Works Corporation shares changed hands at £1 each. The Linton's clerk who sold the shares, one Sidney Taylor, expressed surprise to Shackleton after the deal went through, that Rowe & Pitman had made no attempt to bargain over the share price. He had expected to be beaten down but the price was accepted without discussion. Shackleton, however, would not have been in the least surprised as he had ensured there would be no haggling.

Shackleton had pulled off a neat trick. He had succeeded in convincing Cox's Bank that there was a market for Montevideo shares and, therefore, that his collateral was good. He had also pocketed £5,000 into the bargain because the shares sold to Gower had belonged to him. He had defrauded Gower out of the money on the pretext that he was buying lucrative shares and he had then benefited from the transaction. Not only had he extricated himself from severe difficulties but he had also made a tidy profit in the process.

His good fortune couldn't last indefinitely and his first bad break was the worst. The Mexican scheme at the centre of his complex dealings collapsed. The firm of stockbrokers that had been handling the timber deal had been initially confident. They had sent a representative to Mexico to check the bona fides of

the businessmen behind the enterprise and he had returned satisfied that the investment was sound. But, on 7th May 1910, the
brokers wrote to Shackleton stating that 'owing to a variety of
circumstances, of which the death of King Edward was by no
means the least, [we have] decided to cancel the underwriting of
the Mexican Company's shares'. They were extremely apologetic,
realised that Shackleton had put a lot of hard work into the deal
and that, up until very recently, it had looked like being successful.
The reference to the death of King Edward VII was not elaborated upon. However, there would be more than a touch of poetic
irony if the death of the monarch had precipitated the collapse
of Shackleton's financial house of cards.

The shock to Shackleton's system probably contributed to his
falling ill with appendicitis, which almost killed him. During his
enforced absence from his businesses, things began to slide still
further. He made a trip to America in June 1910 to try to borrow
money from a relative. His efforts were futile and, on 21st July, an
order of bankruptcy was entered against him. The action came
as a blow not only to him, but to the three people whose fortunes
were bound up with his own. Frank Hird and Josephine Browne
were in court on 10th August, the day of his insolvency hearing.
Shackleton was declared bankrupt with debts of almost £85,000.
A measure of penitence might have been expected, but was not
forthcoming. After giving his evidence, Shackleton stepped down
from the witness box and walked purposefully over to where Hird
and Miss Browne were sitting. He stood for a few seconds and
grinned at his victims before resuming his seat.

His treatment of Josephine Browne was especially reprehensi-
ble. He had encouraged her to look upon him as a son. After the

insinuations and outright accusations against him of involvement in the Crown Jewels theft, she had been particularly supportive. She wrote to him frequently and her letters often began 'Dear Little Francis'. In one instance she wrote: 'You are very dear to me, and I am very thankful if in any way whatever I can help to smooth your way and make it easier.' Her attitude to her financial loss was one of disappointed and dignified resignation.

Hird, however, was more muscular in his approach. After the bankruptcy hearing, Shackleton left the court with his brother, Ernest, and one of his sisters. Hird chased the trio through some of the adjoining streets, shouting after them, calling Shackleton a thief and tossing a similar epithet after his brother for good measure. He followed this up by sending Ernest Shackleton an abusive and libellous postcard. The explorer sued and Hird apologised. For many years, Ernest Shackleton was to be followed by persistent rumours that his Antarctic explorations were part-financed by his brother's theft of the Irish Crown Jewels and fraudulent stock dealings. In fact, the reverse was true. Ernest was forced to use much of his own money to support his felonious brother.

Most of the money owed by Shackleton was to Cox's Bank. They had allowed their man a certain amount of breathing space, permitting him to build up his huge overdraft on the basis of the Montevideo shares – a luxury they would regret affording him. In early 1911, the Montevideo Public Works Corporation was declared bankrupt with debts of £943,000, an amount that its originators had managed to incur without one square foot of Uruguayan sea being reclaimed or one brick being placed on top of another in the building of a jetty.

So Cox's Bank was forced to turn its attention to the other element of Shackleton's overdraft guarantee. Lord Gower had effectively underwritten Shackleton's borrowings, though he was unaware of their extent, and he now owed the bank more than £60,000. In March 1911, an order for bankruptcy was obtained by Cox's Bank against Gower but, by now, he hadn't a penny to his name. He had lost a fortune with the collapse of the Montevideo Corporation without ever knowing that he was a shareholder. Presumably the bank meant to have his house and anything else they could lay their hands on, but they were frustrated in their efforts in February 1912 when a lenient view of Gower's situation was taken by the courts. It was concluded that Gower was a badly advised innocent and he was granted a discharge from bankruptcy.

Surprisingly, it wasn't until September 1912 that a warrant was issued for the arrest of Shackleton. As is often the case, the indictment related to one of his lesser crimes. He was charged with having fraudulently converted Miss Browne's £1,000 inheritance cheque. But he had long since left the jurisdiction, having wisely accepted a job as far away from England as he could get. He was employed in Portuguese West Africa (now Angola) as a plantation manager. It was a hot, oppressive climate and the work was hard. But it had the advantage of being far out of reach of his English creditors. Or so he thought.

When his whereabouts became known, he was arrested by the co-operative Portuguese police at Hanha in Portuguese West Africa on 31st October 1912. Scotland Yard was informed of his arrest and immediately sent an officer to repatriate him. The man chosen for the task was Detective Sergeant Charles Cooper, who reached Benguela, where Shackleton was being held, on 9th

December. If he expected a hostile or sullen reception from his compatriot, Cooper was in for a surprise – Shackleton almost embraced the burly, bowler-hatted detective when he saw him.

Cooper had anticipated having to apply for the extradition of his prisoner and expected that this would be contested, but Shackleton was quite willing to waive all his extradition rights. 'I'm so glad you've come,' he said. 'I am most anxious to go back and meet the charges.' Shackleton was not enjoying the delights of Hanha. It had not taken him long to exhaust the meagre social resources of the small British community in the area and now he was pining for home. What were a few months in jail compared to a lifetime in the steamy heat of sub-tropical Africa.

On 22nd December 1912, Shackleton appeared before the Resident Magistrate at Lobito. He had been in custody for six weeks and was not thriving on the experience. His incentive to return home to face the music was growing with every day he spent in custody and he formally agreed to return, voluntarily, with Sergeant Cooper.

The two men travelled from Africa to England on board the liner *Grantully Castle*. On 10th January 1913, Shackleton appeared before Mr Curtis Bennett at Bow Street Police Court and was formally charged before being remanded on bail of £2,000. His father, Dr Henry Shackleton, stood surety for half the amount and Shackleton entered into his own recognisance for the other half.

As the case progressed, more charges were added. The crooked accountant Thomas Garlick was indicted along with Shackleton and both men were also accused of defrauding Lord Gower of the £5,000 used in the elaborate deception of Cox's Bank. The case dragged on over the next ten months, ending up in the

Central Criminal Court. There, on 24th October 1913, a verdict of guilty was brought in by the jury after only ten minutes of deliberation. Shackleton was sentenced to jail for fifteen months with hard labour and Garlick to nine.

Shackleton was fortunate in his family. They might, justifiably, have abandoned him at this stage. He was a source of particular embarrassment to his brother Ernest, who was, after his polar expeditions, in line for a knighthood. However, not even he deserted his brother, visiting him in jail on many occasions.

But enough was enough. When Shackleton was released he was given the opportunity of a fresh start by his family, but under an assumed name: Frank Shackleton became Frank Mellor. Ernest got him a job with William Dederich, a German businessman based in London, who was also a polar enthusiast. Shackleton attempted to conceal his stay in prison by explaining that he had recently returned from 'some islands', but Dederich's staff obviously knew more about his background than he suspected. They, very consciously, never brought up 'the rumoured theft of the Dublin Crown Jewels', observed one of his colleagues, 'we were too tactful'.

Shackleton had always been blessed with artistic talent and impeccable taste when it came to *objets d'art*. He decided to exploit this and opened an antique shop in the crypt of an old Church in South Street in Chichester in Sussex in the 1920s. He advertised in the *Chichester Official Guide* as an 'Antiquary and Genealogist', his specialities being 'old oak furniture, pewter, china and Sussex ironwork. *Pedigrees traced* [my italics]. Coats of Arms painted or engraved'. The cobbler had returned to his last.

A relative, who lived in nearby Eastbourne as a child, remembers

Shackleton as an occasional visitor. He recalls his mother telling him one day, when he was about eleven years old, 'Darling, there's a gentleman coming to see us today, he's a Mr Frank Mellor, but in fact he's your Uncle Frank. Be very polite to him, but if he asks to borrow money, don't give him any.'

Francis Richard Shackleton Mellor, to give him his full, amended name as recorded on his death certificate, died of cancer of the colon on 24th June 1941. He left no will.

'Murder of Sir Arthur Vicars' – *The Times*, 15th April 1921

In the years following his dismissal, Sir Arthur Vicars became increasingly embittered. He talked much of embarrassing the Irish executive but did little about it. He moved to London with a view to establishing a private genealogical practice but nothing came of that venture – though the pretence that the enterprise was about to get off the ground at any moment was kept up. It was a convenient way of maintaining a spirited front for others and of deluding himself.

His state of mind is apparent from his correspondence with his friend James Fuller, the official architect of the Church of Ireland. His letters would deal with genealogy and other matters of mutual interest before wandering off on a meandering course of recrimination in which the chief ogres were Shackleton, MacDonnell, Birrell, the King and the Liberal administration. 'Wait until the unionists come in and I will go for the whole damned lot,' he once wrote.

He never relented in his onslaught against his erstwhile friend. 'Shackleton,' he wrote to Fuller, 'when he was suspected, worked the alleged scandal for all he was worth and even blackened his own character! Threatening to produce a social scandal and involve high persons – none of whom I even knew. This is what prevents my getting justice. I can't ventilate my grievances for the press and parliament have both been "got at" – it only shows the wicked injustice and consequences of blackmail. Shackleton knew the deadly force of the weapon he wielded – but are the government going to encourage such tactics?'

In 1912, Vicars' situation eased somewhat. His circumstances improved, the need to maintain the pretence of setting up a private practice diminished and he was able to return to Ireland. His half-brother, George Mahony, had died and Mahony's home in Kilmorna, County Kerry, had passed to Vicars' sister who generously offered him the use of the place for as long as he wanted. So, he returned to Ireland and settled into semi-retirement in Kerry, but he did not remain in seclusion for long.

The *London Mail* was a sort of Edwardian gossip sheet that specialised in scandal, the nastier the better. It was particularly keen on exposing the sexual peccadilloes of the titled and rich for the edification of its readers. On 23rd November 1912, it published a bizarre story that purported to be an account of the theft of the Crown Jewels. According to the piece, the theft was part of an elaborate scheme of revenge against Vicars, concocted by a lady whom he had crossed in love. Rather than reveal the identity of the lady, Vicars had maintained a studious silence about the whole affair 'at the cost of his post and honour'. The *Mail* wanted to know why: '…those officials all enjoying the highest posts in the

Irish administration, had remained mute through the whole affair, allowed the word "robbery" to be bruited about and yet all the time knew that the jewels were never off the Castle premises? And as a last query, that wants a great deal of explaining: why did Lord and Lady Aberdeen display such extraordinary vindictiveness against Sir Arthur Vicars when their son, Lord Haddo, did all he could to vindicate the accused man?'

Vicars sued the *London Mail* for libel on 28th November. On 14th January 1913, the paper defended itself by claiming that the alleged libel was in fact true. Having done this, it was obliged to justify each of the references made to Sir Arthur. These were delivered to Vicars' solicitors on 31st March 1913 and made even more fascinating reading than the original piece. The *Mail* claimed, in relation to the safe key that:

> *It is the fact that the said key or a skeleton thereof in wax was obtained at some date prior to the removal of the jewels hereinafter mentioned, by a woman going by the name of Malony, commonly known as Molly, but who is now known by the name of Madame Robinson. It is the fact that some of the Crown Jewels were removed by some person from the said safe. It is the fact that previous to the removal of the said jewels at dates which the defendants are unable more particularly to specify, the said woman had acted as and was in fact the mistress of the plaintiff.*

The justification became more bizarre as it went on. Vicars, according to the particulars of justification advanced by the *Mail*, had then begun an affair with Lady Haddo and 'Molly' had become insanely jealous. The night before the theft, Vicars had some visitors in Dublin Castle, among them was the dubious Molly, Lord Gower and Frank Shackleton. A game of cards had begun in the course of which Vicars and Molly had retired and Sir Arthur had 'occupied the same bed during the night with the said woman'. The following morning Molly made for Paris with the jewels and Vicars made no attempt to stop her. Vicars then shielded his paramour before the Commission of Inquiry. At least the penultimate sentence is undoubtedly true. It reads: 'It is the fact that the said woman was not summoned to give evidence before the said Commission.' No doubt, the inquiry was all the duller for her absence.

The particulars of justification were, of course, patently absurd. The story was ludicrous, the role of accomplished sexual athlete did not suit Vicars. Lady Haddo barely knew him socially and 'biblically' not at all. Gower had never set foot in Dublin Castle.

The case was heard on 4th July 1913, five years to the day since the publication of the New York *Gaelic American* claims that had gone unchallenged. The setting was the King's Bench Division and the court was presided over by Justice Darling. The defendants were the Lonmail Syndicate, publishers of the *London Mail*, and the defence was that the allegations were true in substance and in fact, that the opinions expressed were fair comment, made in good faith and without malice upon facts which were a matter of public interest. Claiming justification, defending the original allegations and compounding the libel in the 'particulars of justification' left the *Mail* wide open to severe damages.

Representing Vicars, once again, was the doughty James

Campbell. This time, he was not to be denied his opportunity to defend his client. Unfortunately for Campbell, however, he was interrupted in the middle of his opening address by counsel for the defendants and told that the *Mail* did not propose to justify any of the statements that had been made. They accepted that Vicars and Lord and Lady Haddo had been libelled. It was no contest.

Campbell continued his outraged oration anyway, insisting that those cited or libelled were entitled to their 'day in court'. Vicars and Lord and Lady Haddo were called to give evidence and refuted all the allegations that had been made either in the original story or in the subsequent particulars of justification. In his summing up for the benefit of the jury that was to fix damages, Justice Darling referred to the *Mail* in the most scathing and acerbic terms. The jury was out for only nine minutes, found that Vicars had indeed been libelled and awarded him £5,000.

It all seems just a little too incredible to be true. What lay behind the outrageous libel of the *London Mail*, which was subsequently aggravated by the risible particulars of justification? Was there a hint contained in a letter, sent in 1909, by Vicars to his friend James Fuller? 'If you want to aid me, you will try to get someone to slander me to you and thus enable me to get into a court of law when I can bring the whole thing out.'

Vicars and his allies had felt cheated of their 'day in court' by the terms of reference of the viceregal commission. The *London Mail* libel could have been a ploy to engineer a hearing of the case. In addition, Vicars was almost penniless, his pride had not permitted him to accept the charity of Pierce O'Mahony. The use of Kilmorna was a different matter, it was family property. But he needed money. Victory in a libel suit would have been an elaborate way to circumvent his scruples about accepting charity but, if the libel was gross enough, it would assure him of a sum of money sufficiently large to secure his future.

It is possible, therefore, that the libel was concocted between O'Mahony and the *London Mail* with a guarantee from Vicars' half-brother to defray the costs and damages incurred. It is interesting that all the stock Vicars 'hate' figures feature in the particulars of justification, Shackleton, Gower and, to an extent, Haddo. It is also significant that Vicars is only seriously libelled in reference to his sexual relationship with a woman and the extremities to which he is driven to protect that woman. This portrays Vicars as a noble gentleman who had sacrificed himself for the woman he loved, a veritable folk hero – and a heterosexual folk hero at that.

On the debit side of this argument is the involvement of Lady Haddo. Would O'Mahony have dragged her into the affair? But, in fact, her name is not mentioned at all in the original libel, merely in the particulars of justification, which did not become public until the case was actually heard and the paper admitted that the whole thing was a fabrication anyway. Secondly, Lady Haddo was an object of some gossip in her own right, she was depicted by some as a social climber who had nabbed a title. Her marriage to Lord Haddo in 1906 was her second. Her first had been to a Sheffield draper named Cockayne, who had died leaving her very wealthy. But, as was pointed out, rather gratuitously, in an edition of the *Complete Peerage*, when she had married her first husband, Haddo was only two years old. Perhaps O'Mahony felt that this was a lady who would be quite capable of taking care of herself.

The existence of some sort of benign conspiracy to give Vicars' case an airing while guaranteeing him a measure of financial security is unproven and, probably, unproveable. But the fact remains that, thanks largely to the sum won from the *Mail*, Vicars was able to spend the last years of his life in relative comfort after the financial strains of the years since his dismissal from office.

Indeed, encouraged by the success of the libel action, Vicars was willing to make one last attempt to force some concession from the Irish government six years after the events that had brought about his undoing. O'Mahony wrote to Birrell much along the usual lines, alleging that 'a secret report was set on foot by the Irish government and a report furnished to his late Majesty King Edward, including most baseless insinuations against my brother'. Where this letter differed from others was that it contained an apology from O'Mahony to Birrell because in the past he had 'used expressions regarding your personal conduct in the matter which, on calmer reflection, I consider were not justified'.

Through the Chief Secretary's office, Vicars then petitioned King George V for a public inquiry. The petition was accompanied by a recommendation from Birrell, that it be denied. O'Mahony's piece of self-abasement had been ineffective. The King, however, was not familiar with the history of the case and, unaware of his father's animosity towards Vicars, viewed the case on its merits. He was inclined to agree that Vicars had been harshly treated and was prepared to grant his request. His good intent, however, was unable to withstand a concerted campaign from the Home Office and the office of the Chief Secretary for Ireland who persuaded him to deny the petition. Vicars had finally run out of rope.

On 4th July 1917, at the age of fifty-three, Vicars defied logic, *anno domini*, and a lifetime of bachelorhood, by marrying. His wife was Gertrude Wright, daughter of a Yorkshire doctor, John J Wright, and the older sister of Pierce Gun Mahony's widow, Ethel.

Vicars' next three years were spent in relative calm. He no longer had any financial worries and had long since abandoned any hope of obtaining redress from the government. However, his tranquillity did not last as the peace of Kilmorna was brutally shattered by the onset of war.

During the War of Independence, the IRA's military campaign included attacks on the Anglo-Irish 'big houses' whose owners were mainly unionist landowners and (according to the IRA) potential informers who had no sympathy whatsoever with the aims of the independence movement. Kilmorna was a target for two such attacks. It was in a remote part of the country and was vulnerable to almost anyone who cared to prey on it.

In May 1920, Vicars and his wife were asleep when they heard a loud knocking on the front door. Vicars went down to see what was going on and saw a group of men standing outside. Somebody shouted through the door, demanding to be let in. Vicars refused to open it. The raiders proceeded to break down the door. Once inside, they demanded the keys of Vicars' strong-room, but he refused to hand them over. At that, the leader of the raiders ordered his men to line up in firing-squad formation. Vicars was placed against a wall and the leader began to count. He reached three and then stopped. Vicars still refused to tell the men where the keys were hidden but he agreed to bring them to the strong-room itself. They then tried to break down the strong-room door, but it wasn't as simple a proposition as the front door, and it wouldn't give way. After wasting their energy for a while, the raiders became discouraged and left.

Vicars displayed great personal courage in calling the bluff of his attackers, who were never identified. According to a well-researched article that appeared in the 25th July 1997 edition of *The Kerryman* by Noel Twomey, those responsible were members of the local Duagh Company of the IRA. They were not finished with Vicars yet. As far as the IRA was concerned, he was too friendly with British officers from the Listowel Barracks, whom he regularly entertained at Kilmorna.

On the morning of 14th April 1921, Vicars was in bed recovering from an illness. He was discussing business with the manager of the Kilmorna estate when his wife entered the bedroom. She told her husband that the house had been surrounded by a group of armed men. Afterwards, the estate manager gave an account of what happened.

> *I went to the window and saw two men each carrying two revolvers. I told Sir Arthur to get dressed at once and went downstairs to secure the doors. Two of the raiders were near the back door talking to the valet and the cook — one of these men said, 'It's all right, we've only come to burn the house.' I replied that I was sorry but that I hoped no lives would be taken. He replied that he would guarantee no lives would be lost and held his hand out to me.*

The manager then dashed upstairs and informed Vicars what was happening. Vicars told him that they needed to gather up as many of the valuable possessions in the house as they could carry. The two men then began systematically to strip the house of anything of value and pile the objects outside the front door. The rescue of the valuables was stopped by one of the raiders who placed the manager under guard. Someone spotted Vicars still attempting to save what he could. Up to half a dozen men then followed him down the terrace steps outside. If there was an argument, it was short. The estate manager's account of what happened to Sir Arthur would suggest that there was premeditation. Shortly after they had followed Vicars outside, the raiders shot and killed him. He was still wearing his dressing gown.

By now the house was in flames and the smoke from the fire was spreading. The estate manager, who had been ordered to go over to the tree where Vicars' body lay, became apprehensive. As he walked away from the house, a large cloud of smoke blew across him. He took advantage of the cover it afforded him and made good his escape.

When Vicars' body was found, it had a label round the neck which read: 'Spy. Informers beware. IRA never forgets.' There have been allegations that Vicars was indeed an informer but *Kerryman* writer Noel Twomey offers another reason for the assassination of the unionist, but relatively apolitical, Vicars. He suggests that the attack could have been an act of revenge for the death the previous week in an ambush of young IRA volunteer Michael Galvin, who had been killed by British troops ambushed after a visit to Kilmorna House.

Even from beyond the grave, Vicars' accusations against Shackleton continued. Part of Vicars' will was not admitted to probate in 1922 because he took advantage of this last opportunity to renew his, oft repeated, allegations. The particular part of the will excluded from probate was to have remained closed off until

2022, but an application was made in 1976 to have it opened. The result was no surprise to those familiar with Vicars:

> *I might have had more to dispose of had it not been for the outrageous way in which I was treated by the Irish government over the loss of the Irish Crown Jewels in 1907, backed up by the late King Edward VII whom I had always loyally and faithfully served – When I was made a scapegoat to save other departments responsible and when they shielded the real culprit and thief Francis R Shackleton (brother of the explorer who didn't reach the South Pole). My whole life and work was ruined by this cruel misfortune and by the wicked and blackguardly acts of the Irish government.*

Vicars had enjoyed a certain amount of peace and contentment during his final years. But, as is evidenced by his will, he was not prepared to be magnanimous, even at the end of his life and never truly reconciled himself to the loss of his office – a loss he probably deserved. But the prelude to, and aftermath of, his dismissal reflected little credit upon those who made the decision to end his career.

A week after his death, the *Church of Ireland Gazette* published an anonymous poetic tribute to him. The skill of the poet did not quite match up to his or her heartfelt sentiments. The verse ended thus.

> *Thy honour was unsullied, pure as gold;*
> *Thy courage dauntless, yea, a thousand fold;*

Thy life, thy worship upright, true and clean.
And thou was slain with horrors multiplied,
Like some offending brute led forth and shot
By ruthless hands, no helper at thy side
To soothe the anguish of thy soul distraught.
The land defiled with cruelty and wrong
Utters its bitter cry; Oh, Lord, How Long?

10

Aftermath

THE ORDER OF the Knights of St Patrick was an anachronism
by 1922. The Statutes of 1905 stipulated that the Lord Lieutenant
was the Grand Master and the Chief Secretary, the Chancellor
of the Order. Both government posts had, of course, passed into
history with the signing of the Anglo-Irish Treaty in 1921. In
addition, the knights were dying off rapidly. In 1924, there were
twenty-two; by 1927, only fifteen remained. But the Order was
still very much alive to King George V.

   The monarch wanted to confer the Order of St Patrick on the
Prince of Wales (later King Edward VIII) and on the Duke of
York (later King George VI). To go through with their investitures
would, however, throw down the gauntlet to the new Free State
Government which was unalterably opposed to any revitalisation
of the Order. In the mid-1920s, the Earl of Granard, a much-
respected Knight who had been suggested as a possible Governor
General in 1922, became an intermediary between the monarchy
and the Irish government of W T Cosgrave.

A dialogue continued until 1927 between Granard and Cosgrave. After having survived the initial political and military traumas of independence, the Free State Government had settled into something approaching normality. Thus, issues such as the future of the Knights of St Patrick could now be described in official circles as 'urgent'. The matter was important enough to come up at a meeting of the Executive Council (Cabinet) on 30th March. The Attorney General, John A Costello, was instructed to prepare a report on the Order of St Patrick and its status within the Irish Free State, but, before the Executive Council could consider that report, something far more germane to the principal subject of this book had occurred.

In 1908, James Weldon was a young man in his twenties building up a reputation for himself as a buyer and seller of gems and precious metals for Kelly's of Fleet Street, just behind the Bank of Ireland in College Green. He was the son of a farmer from Kilcock, County Kildare, and had come to Dublin early in life prepared to enter virtually any trade that would have him. That he chanced to fall among jewellers was his good fortune – he proved to be exceptionally able at his job and died a rich man in 1950.

He trained 'on the job', learning the value of the finery in which he dealt by simply buying and selling it. Occasionally, he would lose out on a transaction, but would learn from the experience. At one sale, he lost out to the rival Wine family when one of them distracted his attention at a crucial point in the bidding. Some time later, a very fine silver gilt plaque came up for auction.

One of the members of the Wine family rather foolishly alerted Weldon to their interest in the piece. He was asked not to bid as they wanted to 'buy it for a customer'. Magically, Weldon produced a customer of his own for whom possession of the plaque was imperative. The bidding began. The two dealers between them bid the price up to four times the actual value of the plaque until Weldon, reluctantly, pulled out and the Wines had their piece. Their annoyance at their adversary for the exorbitant price they'd had to pay for the plaque multiplied tenfold when they discovered that it had belonged to Weldon himself!

Like most jewellers, Weldon's employers possessed some fine silverware that was available for hire at dinner parties where the host's own collection was smaller than the number of invited guests. As Kelly's had little confidence in the inclination of the borrowers to count the spoons before the guests left, Weldon was frequently despatched to, among other places, the Viceregal Lodge, to ensure that neither the Lord Lieutenant nor any of his intimates had decided to augment their private collections with Kelly's silver cutlery.

Weldon, although not permitted to mingle at these soirees, succeeded in seeing and being seen, knowing and being known. It may have been coincidence, or he may have been singled out because of his familiarity but, some months after the theft of the Crown Jewels, he was approached in Kelly's by a man who was anxious to raise money on a set of precious gems. Weldon was not allowed to see what was on offer and this fact, allied to the demeanour of the customer, made him suspicious. He reported the approach to the police and gave them a description of the man. Their response was an odd one – they invited him to a ball at Dublin Castle! He was to mingle with the guests and see if he could recognise his mysterious visitor. He did as he was asked, but failed to identify the suspicious customer.

Sometime around 1908–09, Weldon received a letter that astonished him. It was unsigned but the writer claimed that he had possession of the Castle Jewels and asked Weldon to find out from the Guinness family whether or not they would be willing to pay for their return. (Apparently, the family had offered a £10,000 reward for the return of the jewels, though this has never been verified. This amount was well in excess of the government's offer and could have caused problems if it had been publicised.)

Logically, the Guinness family, even if the story of a reward is inaccurate, was the one to approach if a ransom was to be extracted. Apart from the family's wealth, there was a history of philanthropy – Sir Benjamin Guinness had personally paid for the restoration of St Patrick's Cathedral in the 19th century and Edward Guinness, later 1st Earl of Iveagh, had become a Knight of St Patrick in 1895. Iveagh had already spent a small sum of money on the refurbishment of the Office of Arms.

Weldon approached a representative of the family and discovered that they were still prepared to pay a reward for the return of the jewels. His anonymous correspondent had supplied a poste restante address to which he wrote with this information. He received an immediate reply and it is, at this stage, that the affair takes on the appearance of a Victorian cloak-and-dagger melodrama.

Weldon's instructions came either from someone with an overactive sense of caution or a flair for the dramatic. He was to take the boat to England and the train to Euston Station in London.

From Euston, he was to take a cab to a certain point along Hampstead Road. There he was to get out and take a tram to an adjacent street. From there, he was to walk to a particular address and wait outside until someone came and got him. He was to loiter without obvious intent outside the address exhibiting no interest whatsoever in the house or its inhabitants.

Weldon followed the instructions to the letter. He waited outside the meeting place, enabling those inside to have a look at him and ensure that he had not been followed. He had not informed the police of what he was doing, so he was not under surveillance. He stood, with his back to the house, gazing across the street with studied nonchalance. After a few minutes, he felt a tap on his shoulder and heard a voice.

'Mr Weldon?'

He turned. 'Yes,' he replied.

The man who had addressed him did not identify himself. 'Come with me please,' he said.

Weldon followed. Once inside the house, the man explained that he did not have the jewels in his possession, they were locked in a safe in Dublin, but explained that he knew where the safe was and that he had a key. The arrangement was that, when the money was about to be handed over, he would go to Dublin himself and organise the transfer of the jewels.

Weldon returned to Dublin and awaited developments. He heard nothing and it would be almost twenty years before contact was renewed. But the jeweller had recognised the man behind the elaborate subterfuge as Francis Shackleton.

Shortly after his London experience, Weldon left Kelly's and set up an establishment of his own in George's Street, later he moved to Marlborough Street when those premises became too small. At around that time, Weldon got to know W T Cosgrave who introduced him to Michael Collins. Collins, as Minister for Finance in the illegal Sinn Féin Provisional Government, began to make use of the association. As a jeweller, Weldon was constantly banking large sums of money after major sales that would be withdrawn just as quickly when sale was followed by purchase. During the period of the War of Independence, Michael Collins moved about Dublin surprisingly freely for one whom the British authorities were so enthusiastic to interview. His freedom of movement, however, did not extend to lodging and withdrawing money from banks on a regular basis to fund the activities of the Provisional Government. So Collins used Weldon as one his many 'bankers'. He knew that the lodgement and withdrawal of large sums of money within short periods of time by Weldon would be unlikely to attract much attention.

By the mid-1920s, Weldon was prosperous, plump and dapper and had become a firm friend of W T Cosgrave. They were near neighbours in Rathfarnham and met frequently in a social context. It was at this time that the Crown Jewels re-entered Weldon's life. His rather melodramatic tryst in London twenty years previously had almost been forgotten when, at the beginning of 1927, he received another letter concerning the Crown Jewels. This one was as extraordinary as the earlier one in 1908–09 and purported to come from the same person. However, while the first letter had been anonymous, this one was not – it bore the signature of Francis Shackleton. The letter reminded Weldon of the earlier correspondence and the meeting in London which had arisen out of it. Once again, the writer was offering to identify the location of the jewels but, this time, the price being asked for the information had plummeted (particularly taking inflation into account) to £3,000.

Weldon took the proposal seriously enough to visit Cosgrave. Cosgrave's response was typical of his bluntness. 'They're ours anyway, so we might as well have them,' he is reported to have said. (Obviously Mr Cosgrave did not consult the Attorney General for a judgement on the provenance of the jewels. By no stretch of the imagination were they 'ours'. If they were still intact then, and if by some amazing chance they survive to this day, they belong – lock, stock and trefoil – to the British monarchy.) Accordingly, Weldon replied to the forwarding address. Once again, this time finally, the rest was silence.

The Weldon story is based on anecdotal evidence from family and from his close friend, the late Fr Patrick Tuohy. Weldon's daughter, Mrs Clare Williams, now in her nineties and living in Northumberland, remembers the 1927 letter being kept for many years in a wardrobe drawer in her father's bedroom. Sadly, it no longer survives. The first Shackleton letter to Weldon has gone missing as well. He may have handed it over to the DMP or Scotland Yard but it has not turned up in any police file. The only surviving documentary evidence for any of the above comes in a fascinating scrap of paper in the file … the Free State Government kept on the Office of Arms (S3926) from 1927.

IV

OFFICE OF ARMS

The President would like to know exactly what is our position in regard to the Office of Ulster King of Arms.

A proposal was made some years ago by Lord Granard that the Order of the Knights of St Patrick should be revived but the President showed him the undesirability of doing so and the matter dropped.

He would not like them to be used either as a means of reviving the Order or to pass into any hands but that of the State.

V

He understands that the Castle jewels are for sale and that they could be got for £2,000 or £3,000. He would be prepared to recommend their purchase for the same reason.

M.McD
[McDunphy – Executive Council secretary]

1.6.27

There are some intriguing puzzles about this document. Paragraph V is a clear reference to the Crown Jewels and to the offer that came through Weldon. However, just as clearly, the 'them' of paragraph IV does not refer to the jewels. The operative phrase in V is that Cosgrave would be prepared to recommend the purchase of the jewels 'for the same reason' as he would not like 'them' of paragraph IV to pass into the wrong hands, i.e. that both might be used as a pretext for the revival of the Knights of St Patrick, to which, as we have already noted, the Irish government was completely opposed.

So what does 'them' of paragraph IV refer to if not to the jewels?

The most likely candidate is the collection of records and documents of an heraldic and genealogical nature stored in the strong-room of the Office of Arms. The office itself, unlike all others branches of the British administration in Ireland, still remained in British hands. These documents were not just of concern to a few titled families but were the basis of the genealogical history of Ireland. The Free State Government looked upon the documents as 'part of the public records of the country' and still valued them.

The second possibility is that the Irish government coveted the regalia that had not been cleaned out by the Crown Jewel thieves in 1907 – i.e. the Sword of State and two maces. This is less likely unless they were to be displayed as museum pieces. T M Healy, once a defender of Sir Arthur Vicars and now the Governor General, was entitled to use the regalia on state occasions, but he himself loathed the kind of ceremony associated with the years of British rule. However, despite that association, they were part of the heritage of the new Irish nation and the Free State

Government would not want them to fall into the wrong hands, i.e. 'any hands but that of the State'.

During all that passed between Weldon and Cosgrave and his cabinet colleagues, the British were blissfully unaware of the fact that a foreign power might be attempting to buy back part of Britain's patrimony from a convicted swindler. King George V, however, had not been idle. On 3rd June 1927, the *London Gazette* was pleased to announce that the King had appointed His Royal Highness the Prince of Wales, KG, KT, GCSI, GCMG, GCIE, GBE, MC to be a Knight of the Most Illustrious Order of St Patrick. Now all the Prince needed to complete his set was a Bath (Order of).

However, despite the continued efforts of Lord Granard to persuade the Irish government to allow the appointment of new Knights of St Patrick who were not members of the British royal family, the Executive Council, on foot of a report from Attorney General John A Costello, decided on 21st May 1928 'that the Order, now being moribund, should be allowed completely to disappear'.

Lord Granard was informed of the proposed demise of the Order by Cosgrave. London responded with a letter, sent through Granard, indicating simply that the views of the Irish government in respect of the order 'are in several of their respects not shared by His Majesty's Government in Great Britain'. There the matter rested. Two more non-Irish knights were created (the Duke of Gloucester and the Duke of York) but, effectively, the Irish government got its way. No attempts were made to appoint any new Irish Knights of St Patrick.

In 1974, when the Duke of Gloucester died, the Most Illustrious Order of St Patrick died with him.

Epilogue

Who Stole the Irish Crown Jewels?

> *'It is an old maxim of mine that when you have excluded the impossible, whatever remains, however improbable, must be the truth.'*
>
> 'The Adventure of the Beryl Coronet' from
> *The Adventures of Sherlock Holmes* by Sir Arthur Conan Doyle

OF COURSE, WITHIN a matter of days of their disappearance, everyone in Dublin knew who had stolen the Irish Crown Jewels, how and when it had been done and how much the baubles had fetched on the black market. The fact that no two stories tallied only added to the enjoyment. In workplaces, bars and on the streets, favoured candidates for the role of criminal mastermind were floated, shot down, retrieved, dusted off, reflated and advanced once again somewhere else.

In the years since the robbery, various theories – informed, dubious and plain deluded – have been advanced as to the identity of the robbers and the fate of the jewels. It is worthwhile outlining some of these and assessing their relative merits.

Some believe that the jewels ended up in the hands of their ultimate owner. It was remarked upon by many that King Edward VII only became aware that the jewels actually belonged to the British royal family in the course of his first official visit as monarch to Ireland in 1903. It has been suggested that the King saw the rise of the Home Rule Party as a threat to the empire and, at the very least, he did not wish to leave the jewels in the hands of any future Home Rule government. In *Jewels*, a fictionalised account of the theft of the insignia, published in 1977, Robert Perrin took this speculation one step further. He hinted that the Brazilian white stones contained in a brooch habitually worn by Queen Elizabeth II might have come from either the Badge or the Star of the Order of St Patrick.

The story was denied by Buckingham Palace. A spokesman said that no such brooch existed. 'The only piece that comes anywhere near it is a necklace. But that was a present from the President of Brazil.'

The theory put forward, instinctively and self-protectively, by Vicars (namely that the theft was the work of professionals) was the first one to be widely believed. The newspapers, in the absence of any solid information, concluded early on that this was what had happened. However, as their sources (mostly police based) began to work for them, this theory gradually slid into the background.

The obvious requirements of a police investigation are to establish motive and opportunity. If both are present in the case of any individual, that individual must be suspected until their innocence can be proven by means of an alibi. In the case of £50,000 worth of diamonds, the motive is clear enough. But where professional thieves were concerned, while the motivation may have been present, the opportunities were limited. No thief would have dreamed of walking into Dublin Castle unless he knew that the jewels were an easy target. Few criminals, even 'Raffles'-type aristocratic thieves, would have had access to that kind of information.

Furthermore, no professional thief would have gone to all the trouble of obtaining a key of the strong-room, use it to open the door, and then leave three gold collars behind in a flimsy glass case. No professional thief would have bothered to get an exact copy of either the strong-room key or the safe key. A wax impression would have been perfectly adequate. Neither, as was emphasised repeatedly by Inspector Kane, would any seasoned criminal waste his time detaching a stray ribbon from the stolen Badge. Furthermore, he wouldn't have neatly folded up the wrappings for the collars and put them back in their boxes. His aim would have been to get in and out of the premises as quickly as possible. The only feasible way in which an outside thief could have been involved would have been with inside help. This insider might have been able to obtain exact copies of keys as easily as wax impressions. Also, the fact of the theft might have been temporarily concealed to allow this person to establish an alibi of some sort.

The inadequacy of the professional-thief theory is unintentionally highlighted by a cartoon in a magazine called *The Leprechaun* published shortly after the crime was committed. It depicts a large, unsavoury-looking man passing under an arch with 'Dublin Castle' emblazoned on it. He is wearing a tatty top hat at a jaunty angle and is carrying a cudgel in his right hand. In his left hand is a box marked 'Sir Arthur's Jewel Case'. Around his neck is a gold collar with a price tag of £4,000 affixed. On his grubby coat, he is wearing the St Patrick Star (with a £30,000 price tag) and Badge (a real snip, priced at a knockdown £16,000). Behind him, looking on unconcernedly, are: a sentry, standing to attention; a uniformed policeman, saluting; and a third person with 'G-man' written on his bowler hat.

The cartoon was designed to satirise the failure of the DMP to protect the jewels. But the level of exaggeration involved only serves to underline the fact that the odds against a professional thief getting away with the Crown Jewels were prohibitive.

Another theory, more popular in later years than at the time of the robbery, was that the theft had been the work of a republican organisation out to make a political point. The first argument against this notion is that if some band of rogue republicans stole the jewels, they didn't exactly make much political capital out of their escapade.

An idea quite like this was put forward in an article in the

Garda Review in August 1976 by the late Sergeant Gregory Allen, former curator of the Garda Museum in the Phoenix Park. Sergeant Allen refers back to the publication in 1904 of Arthur Griffith's book *The Resurrection of Hungary*, in which he points to the success of the system of dual monarchy in the Austro-Hungarian Empire and advocates a similar arrangement between Britain and Ireland. Sergeant Allen then asks: 'Did Arthur Griffith's writings inspire some unknown patriot to seize the Irish Crown Jewels in furtherance of the dream of a dual monarchy?'

If that was the case the dual monarchists must have succumbed to temptation somewhere along the line and broken up the collection for personal gain. Because the jewels certainly did not re-emerge in 1922 when Ireland acquired dominion status.

The republican theory was given a certain amount of credence by a *Sunday Graphic* article that appeared in 1958. The substance of the story, written by Michael Ryan, was that earlier that year an Irishman called Murray, who lived in London, had received a mysterious phone call from someone who gave no name but spoke with an American accent and described himself as an Irish-American. The caller claimed that he knew the where-abouts of the stolen regalia. 'They are in safe keeping in Philadelphia,' he said, 'but many of us Irish-Americans feel they should be back in Ireland where they belong.' He offered to hand them over to Murray for £10,000.

The reason the offer was made to Murray was because he was the leader of a small Irish monarchist group. An arrangement was made for a meeting between the two men in Soho, London. The usual melodramatic touches were added to make the whole thing convincing – Murray was to come alone and identify himself by means of a rolled-up newspaper in his left hand. Murray was sceptical but intrigued in spite of himself. He contacted Ryan who agreed to follow him and observe whatever took place at the meeting.

But the plans went awry. The mysterious caller was watching Murray as he made his way to the meeting place, realised that Ryan was following Murray, and didn't show up. He rang Murray later in the day and told him there would be no meeting, that he had to return to America that evening.

He also told Murray the story of the theft. The jewels had been stolen by Irish patriots to prevent King Edward VII wearing them on his state visit. They had been kept hidden in a loft somewhere in Dublin for seven months after the theft and then moved. It had been intended to give them back, but constant police activity had made this impossible so, instead, they had been taken to America.

The story isn't very plausible. Leaving aside the fact that the jewels were not intended to be worn by the King at all, but by the Lord Lieutenant, if it was possible to smuggle them to America, it would have been even simpler to return them to the authorities. If the Irish-American caller was sincere in his efforts to restore the jewels to the royalist group (for a price of course), why did he only begin negotiations a matter of hours before he was due to return home to America? The incident has all the hallmarks of a hoax or an unsubtle confidence trick.

It is more than matched for implausibility by the story that appeared in the *Sunday Independent* in September 1976 suggesting that the jewels had turned up in America in 1925. 'Where they had come into the hands of one Mick Finnegan, an Irish patriot.

He was said to have bought them for his old mother Bridget, also known as Brooklyn Bridget.'

Even more recently, on 26th September 1983, a woman walked into the offices of the *Irish Press* newspaper in Burgh Quay in Dublin. She said she wanted to talk to a reporter. Journalist Stephen Collins, then a young reporter, listened with interest to the story she had to tell.

She was in some distress. Her father had just died and she had not really got over the shock. But something had been preying on her mind, something she wanted to talk about. The death of her father had released her from a vow of silence. She told Collins that her grandfather had been involved in the theft of the Irish Crown Jewels. He had been an active republican all his life and, in 1907, he and some of his colleagues had perpetrated what she called 'the crime of the century'. They had stolen the Lord Lieutenant's jewels from under the noses of the police in Dublin Castle.

After the theft, the jewels had been taken to a jeweller in Camden Street before being brought to a farm near the Three Rock Mountain in Rathfarnham, Dublin. They had been split up into three lots and buried. One lot had been buried on the land belonging to the woman who was now relating the story. She had been told of the whereabouts of the jewels as a girl, but her grandmother had made her promise not to say anything until after her father died.

To Collins, the woman appeared lucid and intelligent – she was far from being a crank. He advised her to inform the Rathfarnham gardaí and asked her to keep in touch with him. He then checked out her history. She did indeed belong to a family that owned land in Rathfarnham and that came from a republican background. The gardaí took the woman seriously too. They contacted the National Museum, who were more sceptical. After a short investigation, however, museum officials changed their attitude. They were impressed with the amount of detailed information that the woman was able to give them. They agreed to institute a search of the field on the farm where she claimed the jewels had been buried.

A sophisticated metal detector was used but, after five separate sweeps, the museum staff were still unable to locate the jewels.

When it comes to claims that the regalia fell prey to marauding republicans, one point must be borne in mind. In 1907, extreme nationalists were neither as well organised nor as resourceful as they had been in the past and would become again in the near future. The underground Irish Republican Brotherhood would not have concerned itself with the type of sideshow coup that the theft of the insignia would have represented. If some freelancing IRB members had 'liberated' the gems, they would certainly have made great play of the manner in which they had hoodwinked the authorities. They also did not, in 1907, have sufficient inside information to have increased the chances of success from the sort of sympathisers of the post-1916 Rising period whose intelligence information proved so valuable to Michael Collins.

But what if the jewels were stolen by unionists rather than republicans? That is the theory outlined in *Scandal and Betrayal: Shackleton and the Irish Crown Jewels* published in 2002. Written by John Cafferky and Kevin Hannafin, the book concludes by alleging an elaborate unionist conspiracy designed to discredit Aberdeen and the Liberal administration and involving 'at least one of the more senior Castle policemen [Harrel], a high ranking official in the Home Office [unnamed], another high ranking officer in Scotland Yard [unnamed], Chief Inspector John Kane, and a junior Castle policeman who stole the jewels [Kerr].' The thesis goes on to suggest that Shackleton was either bribed or blackmailed into assisting the conspirators and that one of Kane's principal functions was to shield Shackleton from suspicion. The authors further claim that 'the conspirators secretly returned the jewels to the King'.

However, no documentary evidence whatsoever is advanced to support these controversial theories.

The cause of Lord Haddo is also much canvassed. It would appear fairly certain that, on at least one occasion, he misappropriated the insignia as a practical joke. The argument goes that there was nothing to prevent him repeating the exercise for real. However, it is not a very compelling argument. When Haddo removed the jewels as a prank, he became a marked man; he was seen doing it. Too many people were aware of what had happened and there were just too many good reasons for him not to take the risk of repeating the exercise for profit.

The persistent rumours that went around Dublin, highlighted by Shackleton in his evidence before the Commission of Inquiry, that Haddo had stolen the jewels, were a product of Haddo's past involvement. It was also suggested, by the anonymous 'One in the Know' in the *Evening Telegraph* on 1st February 1908, that these stories were 'circulated industriously for political purposes'. It was good policy from the point of view of the Conservative and Unionist Party to have it believed that the son of a Liberal peer and political appointee was a thief.

Reverting to motive and opportunity again, it is clear that Haddo would have been denied the scope to repeat his 'theft' of the jewels. His opportunity would have been severely curtailed. As regards his motive, he had less incentive than most – he was well enough off.

But the most persuasive argument against Haddo as criminal mastermind is that put forward by Birrell when he sprang to his defence in the House of Commons in April 1908: Haddo had been out of the country from March to November or December 1907. He could not possibly have committed the crime himself. He could, though, have been involved in a conspiracy with one or more members of the staff of the Office of Arms. The gap of over four months, between the time of his departure from the country and the discovery of the theft, makes that possibility somewhat less than likely. But it must always remain a possibility.

If we accept the opinion of Inspector Kane – that the theft was committed by someone familiar with the workings of the Office of Arms – then the list of candidates is narrowed considerably. Some of those involved with the office can be eliminated straight-away. Vicars, except for the period immediately after the theft, was never under suspicion. Neither was Burtchaell who, in addition to his patent honesty, was not a well man and was subject to frequent epileptic fits.

Pierce Gun Mahony was not seriously suspected either and was allowed to remain on in the Office of Arms when the other heralds had all been asked to resign. The only doubt about him concerns the violent nature of his death (which could have been an accident, suicide or murder). In any case, his death could have been connected with the theft, but the likelihood is remote.

Francis Bennett Goldney was a man of considerable personal wealth. It is difficult to imagine him getting caught up in any such enterprise as the theft of the insignia. In his case, though one unsolved riddle does remain. In *The Magpie Tendency*, written by local Canterbury historian Audrey Bateman, Goldney emerges as something of a kleptomaniac. After his death, it transpired that, for a Conservative, he had a highly socialistic inclination to appropriate the property of others. He had managed, over the years, to acquire a number of precious objects and documents from a variety of institutions – including antique charters of the City of Canterbury, two chalices from its cathedral and a painting belonging to the Duke of Bedford.

When Vicars had shown the jewels to his friend Hodgson in June 1907, the librarian had been far more interested in seeing a blue velvet garter, also on display in the Office of Arms, that had belonged to the Duke of Marlborough. In 1908, a letter appeared in a local Canterbury paper pointing out what a coincidence it was that a garter belonging to the great Duke should now be on exhibition in the Beaney Museum in Canterbury (of which Francis Bennett Goldney was honorary curator). It was in a glass case bearing the legend 'lent by F B Goldney FSA'. After the letter was published, a number of curious visitors appeared at the museum all expressing an interest in the garter. It was quickly withdrawn from its case though no mention was made of who had removed it or why it had gone. Had Goldney removed the garter from the Office of Arms? Was someone capable of such an act also capable of complicity in a far bigger theft? Possibly, but it is a giant leap from opportunistic pilfering to carefully planned and well-executed larceny.

However, the most persistent and persuasive rumours surrounded the involvement of Frank Shackleton. At the time of the robbery, Shackleton was getting deeper and deeper into debt. His investment in the Mexican Land and Timber Company needed constant topping up if it was to succeed. He was strapped for money, as he revealed to the viceregal commission, but was conducting his affairs as if he was in no difficulties whatsoever.

He took effective control of the financial affairs of Gower, Hird and Josephine Browne in 1907 and so was already involved in criminal activity at the time of the theft. Shackleton clearly had the motivation for stealing the jewels, or at least for borrowing them to obtain ransom. He also knew how vulnerable they were. He had remarked on the lack of adequate security and was presented with all the opportunities that anyone could wish for to prepare the groundwork for the theft. Disarmingly, he admitted to the commission that he had constant access to Vicars' keys and could easily have had copies made of any of them.

One aspect of Shackleton's behaviour that has tended to convince some of his innocence is this very candour. In his evidence before the Commission of Inquiry, he denied that he had stolen the jewels but admitted that he had ample opportunity to do so. His conversation over lunch at Lady Ormonde's when he remarked that he would not be surprised to see the jewels stolen some day is also advanced as evidence of his innocence. Why, it has been asked, would any man, implicated in a theft, draw attention to himself in such a fashion? To this rhetorical question, however, there is an answer. A clever man would anticipate that such a potentially incriminating observation would be more likely to exonerate than implicate him. Simply because he drew attention to the possibility of his own guilt does not mean he was innocent.

James Weldon was in no doubt that the man he met in London some time after the theft, and who offered to tell him where the jewels were, was Shackleton. However, even this does not firmly establish Shackleton's guilt. He was a clever and resourceful man, cunning and unscrupulous enough to turn the rumour and innuendo that surrounded him to his own advantage. A man who was astute enough to convince a bank that totally valueless shares could be sold at par was capable of extracting ransom for a set of jewels that he had never stolen in the first place. The entire exercise could have been a charade, a massive bluff.

When it comes to establishing Shackleton's guilt there still remains one major hurdle, his alibi. Like Haddo, he was out of the country when the theft took place. However, he was gone for only one month. Given the scale and the thoroughness of the police investigation into his movements, it is highly improbable that he slipped back into the country surreptitiously, as Vicars alleged. Therefore, he could not have actually stolen the jewels himself. He could only have expedited matters for an accomplice. This is where Gorges comes in. He was in Ireland at the time of the theft and was acquainted with the layout of the Office of Arms.

Like Shackleton, Gorges was a familiar figure around Dublin Castle. He was also finding it difficult to live on his captain's salary, supplemented by some assistance from his family. He was the kind of man who was used to taking risks. For someone like him, the theft itself would have been child's play. Furthermore, on at least two occasions, he implicated himself in the theft. After reading the *Gaelic American* story, which Bulmer Hobson handed him, he admitted that it was substantially true (though we are left with the disturbing 'Gaudeans' inconsistency). In 1915, while in jail for the murder of Detective Young, he boasted of his part in the crime. In both instances, it might have been a demonstration of the type of bravado to which he was prone. Undoubtedly he wanted to impress Hobson, given the proposition he was about to put to him. Similarly, most prison inmates like to command the respect of their fellow convicts, it makes life inside more agreeable. On that occasion, the police questioned him but they were not sufficiently impressed with his answers to pursue the matter.

The problem with the accusations against both Shackleton and Gorges is that they largely emanate from the same source. The allegations made against them in the *Gaelic American* came, via Hobson, from Vicars and O'Mahony. Shackleton and Gorges were mentioned in the House of Commons by Ginnell, but his information came via the same route. There are hints in the correspondence in the Royal Archive in Windsor Castle between Aberdeen and Knollys that Shackleton was guilty of far more than homosexual activities. But they are only hints.

In 1909, Vicars was certain he had convinced Kane that his theory was correct. He wrote to Fuller that: '...no one knows how Shackleton gets his money – his own family don't know. He bought, since the robbery, an £850 motor car and lives in a huge house, beautifully furnished at 29 Palace Court... He lives in great style. He is wonderfully clever – bamboozles everyone and Kane admits he is very clever and at first entirely threw him off the scent by his cool manner.' However, even if Kane had finally been convinced that Shackleton was the culprit (and we cannot trust Vicars' assertion that this was the case), he clearly had not amassed sufficient evidence against Shackleton to do anything about it. Shackleton's wealth was as likely to have come from the ill-gotten gains of his fraudulent financial activities as it was to have been derived from the proceeds of a jewel robbery.

But if we are to be governed by the maxim of Sherlock Holmes ('when you have excluded the impossible, whatever remains, however improbable, must be the truth'), then we are left with Shackleton as the architect and Gorges as the executor of the crime. On the balance of probability and on the basis of the available documentary and anecdotal evidence, it must be concluded that, at the very least, they are the two men most likely to have committed the theft.

❧

This is how it might have happened.

Shackleton discovered himself in desperate need of money. His brokers were looking for extra financing for the Mexican deal, he owed Cox's Bank close to £40,000 and he had no way of paying either. He needed a once-off, quick, speculative coup. At the same time, he noticed the vulnerability of the Crown Jewels and he realised the potential gains that might accrue from stealing them.

But he knew that his association with the Office of Arms would make him a suspect and that suspicion would deepen when the police investigated his financial affairs, as they invariably would. He needed an alibi. He needed to be out of the country when the insignia were stolen. Therefore, he required an accomplice and, for that, he did not have to look too far. At the time, he was involved in a homosexual relationship with Richard Gorges, who had the qualities of recklessness and daring that made him ideal for such a potentially hazardous enterprise. For the profit involved, he was prepared to take the risks, provided Shackleton simplified things for him. Vicars' keys were duly stolen and copies of both were made by Shackleton before he left for England on 7th June.

The timing of the theft was crucial. Gorges would be in Ireland for a month for the annual militia training. Shackleton knew that, once the Castle season was over, there was very little cause to open the safe and the robbery might go undetected for weeks. If the plan was to work, it was essential that the theft be discovered while Shackleton was out of the country. So Shackleton had to have some guarantee that the safe would be opened and the alarm raised while his alibi stood.

Ironically, it was King Edward himself who provided that

guarantee. The King announced, privately, that he intended to pay a visit to Ireland. The formal announcement was not made until 11th June but, long before that, those who worked in the Office of Arms were well aware that the King was due to begin his visit on 10th July. This was just what Shackleton needed. The safe would have to be opened well before the arrival of the King to prepare the insignia for the official functions at which Aberdeen, as Lord Lieutenant and Grand Master of the Order of St Patrick, would wear them. Shackleton would also be expected to return for the ceremonies that were to form part of the visit. He wanted to leave a decent interval between his own return and the arrival of the King so the jewels would have to be stolen before then.

One night, sometime before 2nd July, Gorges let himself into the Office of Arms. His rank and familiarity allowed him to breeze past the sentry at the Castle gate and gain access to the Bedford Tower with a copy of one of the many latchkeys in circulation. He went straight to the safe, which he opened with a replica key. He carefully extracted the jewels and collars from their boxes, replacing the collar wrappings neatly. He had been warned by Shackleton about the Badge and the blue ribbon that was attached to it. It was just the kind of small detail on which the two men feared they would trip themselves up – they might have, inadvertently, forgotten about the ribbon after disposing of the jewels. There was no point in hanging on to anything that might help tie either of them to the theft. Gorges had come armed with a small screwdriver with which he worked the ribbon loose.

Why he didn't steal anything from the strong-room remains a mystery. He certainly had a key to the room that he used a few nights later. He may well have become uneasy at the length of time it had taken him to manipulate the ribbon from the Badge or he might just have become generally nervous and felt he had outstayed his welcome. The objects that Gorges had stolen were small enough to fit comfortably into the pockets of a greatcoat without leaving the slightest bulge. Having got what he had come for, he left and hid the jewels in some pre-designated spot.

The two then waited for their theft to be discovered. Shackleton needed to return to Dublin a day or two before the arrival of the King and a day or two after the theft of the jewels. But the time passed and there was no sign of any hue and cry. The more time elapsed, the more worried Shackleton became. It was conceivable that the safe would not be opened until the actual morning of the King's visit, by which stage Shackleton would be in Dublin with his alibi blown.

He contacted Gorges and both men agreed that they had no option but to alert the authorities themselves. The most effective way of doing this was also the most hazardous. On the night of 2nd July, Gorges entered the Bedford Tower once again and left the front door on the latch. This was how Mrs Farrell found it the following morning.

But, to their consternation, this move produced no apparent results – no banner headlines in the newspapers announced that the Irish Crown Jewels had been stolen. Shackleton's return to the country was imminent. Gorges was obviously going to have to do something dramatic to attract someone's attention in the Office of Arms. On the night of Friday 5th July, he broke into the Bedford Tower for the third time. He went to the safe again and opened it. He left it unlocked, but closed over and with the handles in the locked position. Then he headed for the strong-room.

Here he opened the outer door. He made no attempt to take any-thing from the strong-room and, leaving the door ajar, left. Astonishingly, even after all these elaborations, the theft was still only discovered by accident.

The initial plan had probably been to hold the jewels until a ransom was paid but, with Shackleton under close observation, this was out of the question. So Shackleton began to visit pawn-shops in London. This was one of the reasons the authorities pressed for his resignation as Dublin Herald. He knew he was taking a major risk and stopped when he became aware that the police were following him. He then headed for Paris to try his luck (he told the viceregal commission of at least two trips to the French capital). It is possible that Shackleton was only looking for a temporary resting place for the jewels, collateral for a loan that would tide him over a bad patch. He would return to redeem the gems when the Mexican deal realised the anticipated profit, when his ship came in. Sadly for him it never did.

Whatever money he could have got for the jewels was only a fraction of their true value. After dividing it with Gorges, it was half of that fraction. His portion of the take was soon swallowed up by his financial black hole. To outward appearances, he did not look like a man who had benefited from the proceeds of a huge jewel robbery. In fact, the money had simply postponed the inevitable collapse of his business interests. Gorges was clever enough not to acquaint all and sundry with the fact of his own new-found wealth. Spun out, the money was enough to keep him for a while after his rupture with the army in 1908 and the curtailment of his income.

It is known that the police strongly suspected both men. It is alleged that they were shielded because they threatened to expose the homosexual activities of a group of aristocrats who included the Duke of Argyll, the brother-in-law of Edward VII. This may very well be true, but there is no evidence to support these claims. It would be rash to assume that, because Shackleton was a homosexual, all his associates must have been as well – and that they too had something to hide.

So, did Francis Shackleton and Richard Gorges steal the Irish Crown Jewels and escape conviction, or even arraignment, because of the threat of blackmail? Did they get away with a major crime because of the damage they could do to members of the British aristocracy close to the monarchy? Does the failure of the authorities to identify and charge the men who stole the Crown Jewels lie in a simple case of noblesse oblige?

The truth behind the apparent immunity of Shackleton and Gorges from prosecution could well be more mundane. The police may simply have not had enough evidence against them. Kane was very specific about this in a statement before the viceregal commission. No tangible evidence was found to incriminate Shackleton.

In the end, all we are left with are theories and questions. In the absence, so far at least, of any conclusive documentary proof, we can only speculate. There may very well be crucial documents related to the Crown Jewels affair lurking in some dingy corner of some unlikely archive. If these emerge in the future, they could shed more light on the affair and identify the thieves. If proof positive does ever emerge, this writer is convinced that it will finally identify Francis Shackleton and Richard Gorges as the conspirators who stole the Irish Crown Jewels.

As long as the Irish Crown Jewels remain undiscovered treasure trove, they will continue to exert a sort of fascination over the Irish psyche. As recently as August 1998, an elaborate hoax was carried out in Kerry when Michael Murphy, a nephew of Vicars' valet, was contacted by telephone by a man 'with a distinct English accent' who instructed him to go to the old garden of Kilmorna House. There, according to newspaper reports, he found a large cast stone slab with a Latin inscription that appeared to have been removed from a wall. A theory current at the time was that a box containing the jewels had been removed from the base of the stone. The discovery was taken seriously enough to be investigated by the gardaí and drew a guarded request from the Keeper of Antiquities at the National Museum for the return of the jewels if, in fact, they had finally been found. As time went on, the whole affair was dismissed as an extremely carefully planned and well-executed hoax. While filming in Kerry in late 2002 for an RTÉ television documentary on the theft of the Crown Jewels, producer Gerry Nelson was contacted by the Kilmorna hoaxer who offered information on the whereabouts of the jewels. Nelson, however, had been told to expect the call and didn't bite.

By now, the Irish Crown Jewels have probably long since been broken up into their constituent parts. The various rubies, diamonds and emeralds could be adorning the fingers, necks or ears of women from Ballivor to Beverly Hills; gold from the collars of the Knights of St Patrick may have been fashioned into heirlooms for a new Irish aristocracy. But perhaps James Weldon was right to shake vigorously every decent-sized safe that came up for auction in Dublin, in the hope that his mysterious 1927 correspondent had not been trying to dupe him after all.

The original safe, from which the jewels were stolen, now sits, largely redundant, in a corner of the lost and stolen property office in Kevin Street Garda Station in Dublin. It bears the legend 'Ratner Safe – Thief Proof'.

A Note on Sources

Research for this book was conducted in the National Library in Dublin, the British Library, the Bodleian Library, the Irish and British Public Records offices, the State Paper Office and the Royal Archive in Windsor.

The most vital and valuable source was the lengthy and exhaustive appendix to the Report of the Viceregal Commission Appointed to Investigate the Circumstances of the loss of the Regalia of the Order of St Patrick (the viceregal commission). This contains over 3,000 questions and answers and, if published in book form, would be longer than this entire account. Most of the fine detail contained in my version of events comes from the mouths of the participants themselves, as told to the three commissioners. In their evidence, they also spoke about their opinions and feelings. So it is possible to get a first hand, personal history without having been able to talk to any of those directly involved in the crime and its aftermath. This would have been a far skimpier volume without the evidence given to the viceregal commission.

Other primary sources included manuscript material from a number of collections. These include:

RA X 13; RA W 75; RA W 28 and RA R 38 from the Royal Archive in Windsor Castle. I would like to acknowledge the gracious permission of Her Majesty the Queen for access to this material.

HO 45/9860; CO 739/21; DO 35/14; DO 35/35; DO 35/61 and DO 117/108 at the Public Records Office in London.

The Home Office allowed me access to their file 156/610/16. This included material relating to the claims by Gorges, from his prison cell, to have stolen the jewels. It does not, however, include the elusive report of Inspector Kane.

That the report existed there is no doubt. The Chief Secretary, Augustine Birrell, confirmed that in an answer to two parliamentary questions. The report itself, however, has disappeared. There must have been at least two copies – one destined for Scotland Yard and a second, which the Chief Secretary's files show was sent to Dublin on 24th January 1908. It is curious that, amid the plethora of material that does survive on the subject to the present day, this vital document is no longer with us. Repeated applications to the Departmental Records Office in Scotland Yard have produced the same response, no such report exists. Neither has it turned up in the British Home Office or the Public Records Office in Kew. It is significant, however, that the file in the Home Office relating to the Crown Jewels case (156,610) has huge gaps. Whole sections have, it would appear, been removed. The result is that the contents of the file have been completely sanitised. As Susan Hood has pointed out in her excellent history of the Office of Arms, *Royal Roots, Republican Inheritance*, a total of eight Home Office files on the 'Larceny of the Crown Jewels' have been destroyed.

In the normal course of events, files are sent to the Home Office from the various British government departments after thirty years. Anything that is extremely sensitive may be kept back completely or may operate under a hundred-year rule.

Home Office File 156,610, to which I was granted access, was not due to be sent to the Public Records Office until 2022. At one stage, it must have contained something worth keeping under wraps for a hundred years, but not any more. It has been filleted of anything remotely controversial.

Much of the official correspondence between the key players in the Irish administration was contained among the large volume of letters in Additional Manuscripts 45,995; 45,985; 46,065; 41,239 and 41,240, which were consulted at the British Library.

Private collections trawled for additional private correspondence were the Chamney Manuscripts at the Genealogical Office in Dublin, and the MacDonnell, Magill and Birrell papers at the Bodleian Library in Oxford.

The files on the theft from the Chief Secretary's Office were stored in the State Paper Office, Dublin Castle, and have now been transferred to the National Archive. The relevant files were: CSORP 11178 (1890); 8317 (1891); 17756/07; 2076/08; 5930/08; 11108/08; 1110/08; 5352/08; 8292/08; 12809/08; 22582/10; 18119/13 and 16820/14.

The fate of the Knights of St Patrick and the offer of the jewels to the government was documented in two Free State Government files from the 1920s: S3926A and S5708.

The will of Sir Arthur Vicars, in which he accuses Shackleton of responsibility for the theft, was consulted in the Public Records Office in the Four Courts, Dublin.

Other printed sources included the memoirs and autobiographies of a number of the major and minor players in the drama as well as those who were not directly involved but who knew (or purported to know) something about the affair.

These included:

Aberdeen, John Campbell (1st Marquess) & Ishbel
    (Marchioness), *We Twa* (London, 1925).
    —*More Cracks With We Twa* (London, 1929).
Birrell, Augustine, *Things Past Redress* (London, 1937).
Blunt, Wilfrid Scawen, *My Diaries* (London, 1921).
Headlam, Maurice, *Irish Reminiscences* (London, 1947).
Hobson, Bulmer, *Ireland, Yesterday and Tomorrow* (Tralee, 1968).
McLysaght, Edward, *Changing Times – Ireland Since 1898*
    (Bucks, 1978).
McNeil, J G Swift, *What I Have Seen and Heard* (London, 1925).
Robinson, Sir Henry, *Memories, Wise and Otherwise*
    (London, 1923).
Wilkinson, Sir Neville Rodwell, *To All and Singular* (London, 1922).

As regards the material in the later chapters, I relied heavily on interviews, some with people who prefer to remain anonymous. I am grateful to Mrs O'Farrell for information on her mother-in-law and to Stephen Collins and Brendan O'Riordan who provided me with all the information confidentiality allows, on the search for the jewels in the early-1980s.

The Weldon material is a synthesis of the memories of his daughter, Mrs Clare Williams, his grandson, James Weldon Jr, and, principally, his good friend and confidante, the late Fr Patrick Tuohy, to all of whom I am indebted.

Another valuable oral source was two tapes in the RTÉ archives in which Eoin 'The Pope' O'Mahony (a member of the O'Mahony /Vicars clan) spoke colourfully (but often inaccurately) about his family's involvement in the affair.

Contemporary newspapers and periodicals were very useful and informative also, *The Irish Times* for the period was the most valuable resource. Also useful were: the Dublin *Evening Mail*, *The Times* (London); the *Pall Mall Gazette*; the *Evening Telegraph*; the *London Opinion* and the New York *Gaelic American*. Information about the declining years of Frank Shackleton came from the Chichester *Official Guide*. The *Church of Ireland Gazette* had a useful obituary of Vicars and the *Police Review* of April 1915 carried an obituary of Inspector Kane.

Good Books at the Beaney, the Quarterly Bulletin of the Canterbury Royal Museum and public library, contained a useful article on Francis Bennett Goldney by J G B Stone.

Secondary sources were, in general, only of interest where they helped towards an understanding of the period in which these events took place. The obvious exception being the most rigorous and objective historical work available on the subject of the Crown Jewels theft, Bamford and Bankes' highly readable and scholarly *Vicious Circle*.

The list of secondary sources consulted includes:

Allen, Gregory, 'The Great Jewel Mystery' *Garda Review* (August, 1976).

Bamford, Francis & Viola Bankes, *Vicious Circle* (London, 1965).

Bateman, Audrey, *The Magpie Tendency* (Canterbury, 1999).

Beckett, J C, *The Making of Modern Ireland* (London, 1969).

Burke's Peerage and Baronetage

Cafferky, John & Kevin Hannafin, *Scandal and Betrayal: Shackleton and the Irish Crown Jewels* (Cork, 2002).

Deale, Judge Kenneth, *Memorable Irish Crimes* (London, 1960).

De Vere White, Terence, *The Anglo-Irish* (London, 1972).

Galloway, Peter, *The Most Illustrious Order of St Patrick* (London, 1983).

Gribble, Leonard, *Great Manhunters* (London, 1966).

Hood, Susan, *Royal Roots – Republican Inheritance: The Survival of the Office of Arms* (Dublin, 2002).

Hyde, H Montgomery, *Cases that Changed the Law* (London, 1951).

Lee, Sir Sidney, *King Edward VIII – A Biography* (London, 1927).

Malloch, Russell J, 'The Missing Regalia of the Grand Master of the Order of St Patrick' *Orders and Medals* (Autumn 1977).

Neligan, David, *A Spy in the Castle* (London, 1968).

O'Broin, Leon, *The Chief Secretary – Augustine Birrell in Ireland* (London, 1969).

Risk, James C, 'The Insignia of the Order of St Patrick' *Orders and Medals* (Winter 1977).

The Kerryman (25th July 1997).

Twomey, Noel, 'The Mystery of the Stolen Crown Jewels'

Who's Who (London, 1906).

Who Was Who 1916–28 (London, 1929).

One of the best abbreviated accounts of the affair is on the website: http://homepage.tinet.ie/sean_murphy/irishmys/jewels.htm.

There is also an interesting account on www.doyle.com.au/order_st_patrick.htm written by Michael Nash (which, *inter alia*, quotes the present author's *Irish Times* article from 1982).

Timeline

🔖 **1893**

Vicars becomes Ulster King of Arms

🔖 **1897**

Shackleton becomes Assistant Secretary in the Office of Arms

🔖 **1899–1902**

Boer War

🔖 **1903**

Office of Arms moves to Bedford Tower

🔖 **1905**

Vicars revises the Statutes of the Order of St Patrick
Aberdeen becomes Lord Lieutenant
Shackleton becomes Dublin Herald
Pierce Gun Mahony becomes Cork Herald

❧ 1907

| February | – Bennett Goldney becomes Athlone Pursuivant |

7th June	– Shackleton leaves Dublin for one month
11th June	– last time jewels seen intact
	– formal announcement of King Edward VII's visit to Ireland

6th July	– Discovery of the theft of the Jewels
7th July	– Kerr's investigation
9th July	– Shackleton returns to Dublin
10th July	– King Edward VII's official visit begins
11th July	– Inspector John Kane of Scotland Yard arrives, tours Dublin Castle and interviews Vicars
16th July	– Kane's initial report to Aberdeen and Scotland Yard

| 28th August | – Lord Aberdeen receives Hadley Street telegram |

| 4th September | – Great Malvern psychic admits sending Hadley Street telegram |

| early October | – Aberdeen, Birrell, MacDonnell, Dougherty, Ross and Harrell meet to decide the fate of Vicars |

23rd October	–	Vicars receives letter from Dougherty effectively dismissing him
2nd November	–	Pierce O'Mahony meets Birrell and Aberdeen
21st November	–	Aberdeen suggests to Knollys that Sir Alexander Porter be asked to investigate the situation at the Office of Arms
late November	–	Porter reports
7th December	–	letter to Vicars from Aberdeen confirming his dismissal
9th December	–	letter from O'Mahony saying Vicars being used as a scapegoat
22nd December	–	Knights of St Patrick petition on behalf of Vicars presented to King Edward
23rd December	–	King Edward refuses establishment of royal commission to investigate the theft of the jewels; Aberdeen suggests viceregal commission as an alternative

❦ 1908

10th January	–	Viceregal Commission of Inquiry under Justice Shaw convenes in the library of Office of Arms, Vicars withdraws from the commission
16th January	–	Shackleton gives his evidence to the viceregal commission
24th January	–	DMP receives Kane's report

26th January	–	copy of the commission's report is sent to Aberdeen
28th January	–	Neville Rodwell Wilkinson is appointed new Ulster King of Arms, replacing Vicars
30th January	–	Vicars learns of contents of commission's report and receives another dismissal letter
31st January	–	official publication date of the commission's report; contents of report appear in newspapers; a letter from Vicars detailing his response to the report is published in *The Irish Times*
1st February	–	Vicars refuses to hand over his keys to the strong-room
2nd February	–	strong-room is partially demolished
17th February	–	'Blue Book of Evidence' from the commission is published
1st April	–	Parliamentary question put down to Birrell to enable him to exonerate Lord Haddo
4th July	–	publication of the Hobson/O'Beirne article in Devoy's *Gaelic American*

✍ 1909

| 27th April | – | Parliamentary exchange between Ginnell and Birrell on 'crimes' committed in Dublin during 1907 |

✍ 1910

February — Josephine Browne gives Shackleton her
inheritance cheque of £1,000

1st March — Shackleton share deal to deflect suspicions
of Cox's Bank is completed

7th May — Stockbrokers foreclose on Shackleton's
Mexican deal

21st July — Order of bankruptcy served on Shackleton

10th August — Shackleton's insolvency hearing, he is
declared bankrupt

✍ 1912

31st October — Shackleton arrested in Portuguese West Africa

28th November — Vicars sues *London Mail* for libel

12th December — Ginnell questions Birrell on Kane's report
22nd December — Shackleton appears before Resident
Magistrate in Portuguese West Africa

✍ 1913

10th January — Shackleton appears at Bow Street Police
Court

14th January	–	*London Mail* defends its comments, libel trial to proceed
16th January	–	Ginnell questions Birrell again on Kane's report, Birrell admits people were named in report
31st March	–	*London Mail*'s justification for its comments delivered to Vicars, insinuates Vicars' affair with Lady Haddo
4th July	–	Vicars' libel case against *London Mail* begins; *London Mail* admits the libel of Lord and Lady Haddo and of Vicars; Vicars receives £5,000
24th October	–	Shackleton sentenced to jail for fifteen months for fraud

❧ 1914

27th July	–	Death from gunshot wounds of Pierce Gun Mahony

❧ 1915

14th July	–	Gorges kills Detective Young, later sentenced to twelve years penal servitude for manslaughter

☙ 1917

4th July   – Vicars marries Gertrude Wright

☙ 1921

14th April   – Vicars killed by the IRA during a raid on his house in Kilmorna, County Kerry

☙ 1927

May   – James Weldon receives a letter offering information on the whereabouts of the Crown Jewels; informs W T Cosgrave

1st July   – Minute of Executive Council meeting refers to the offer of the Jewels and attempts to revive Order of St Patrick

☙ 1928

21st May   – Decision to let the Order of the Knights of St Patrick disappear taken by the Executive Council

☙ 1941

24th June   – Death of Shackleton

Index